The Gospel We Preach

Keith Tipple

ISBN 978-1-64114-757-6 (Paperback)
ISBN 978-1-64114-758-3 (Digital)

Christian Faith Publishing, Inc.
296 Chestnut Street
Meadville, PA 16335
www.christianfaithpublishing.com

Printed in the United States of America

Dedication

I dedicate the writing of this book to my wonderful wife Val who over the years has been a constant source of encouragement and help in our ministry together both in pastoral life, missions and ministry trips. In our early days of ministry, she would often have to stay home and look after our two boys Mark and Paul when I was conducting evangelistic missions or away on ministry trips. She truly is a wonderful co-worker in this glorious gospel we are privileged to preach. She loves the Lord and truly loves to worship Him. It has been my privilege to have her minister alongside me and to see the impact she has upon people when she ministers the word of God.

Thank you Val for encouraging me to write this book, I hope it is a blessing to you when you read it.

Acknowledgment

My sincere thanks to Keith and Ruth West who have helped so much in the initial editing of this book, your encouragement has meant so much to me.

Thanks to our family.

Thank you so much to Mark and Paul our two sons their wives Sian and Melissa and families. For your encouragement love and dedication to the Lord. Never underestimate the love of God that is revealed in this glorious Gospel, and our love and continued prayers for you all.

Thanks to our Pastor
Thank you to my Pastor, mentor and friend Ray Belfield. For the vision you imparted to me, the faith you ministered to me, and the opportunity you gave to me.

Contents

Foreword

I have known Keith and Valerie Tipple for over 50 years. He is a gifted church planter, pastor and evangelist he commenced his ministry as an evangelist on our ministry team at the Wigan Assembly of God church in the UK. which I was pastor of for some 32 years.

Keith and Val are partly supported in travelling to Asia, Singapore and several African Countries by charitable gifts from churches and individuals who support the Ocean-Wings Trust which has 5 trustees here in the UK.

Keith and Val conduct conferences and have exercised considerable faith and wisdom in these affairs. They have returned numerous times to hold conferences and missions and to speak in small and large churches in Uganda where the churches have grown, as a result of such in Kapyani village Uganda 100 have recently been baptized in water on their latest ministry trip.

I count it a privilege and delight to write this simple forward to this book which deserves a wide reading across the world. It will enlighten and bless all who take time to think and digest its contents, respectfully,

Raymond Belfield, Wigan, God has all the Glory!!

Introduction

Heaven opened, God spoke, the Spirit descended, and the announcement was made. "This is my beloved Son in who I am well pleased." These words ushered in a time that would be unparalleled in the history of the world. The seed of the woman promised in Genesis 3:15, through whom all the nations of the world would be blessed, was now standing in the river Jordan, having just been baptized to fulfill all righteousness. The Messiah was ready to commence His ministry upon the earth. Terror must have shot through the caverns of hell. Into a world dominated by the powers of darkness, another Kingdom was coming—the Kingdom of God.

After a period of fasting and prayer in the wilderness, Jesus returned in the power of the Spirit.

It is the Gospel writer Luke who records in the fourth chapter (v. 16) that Jesus returned to Nazareth, His hometown, and, as His custom was, went into the synagogue on the Sabbath day and stood up to read. When He opened the book, He found the place where Isaiah the prophet had written this:

> The Spirit of the Lord is upon me, because He has anointed me to preach the Gospel to the poor; He has sent me to heal the brokenhearted, to proclaim liberty to the captives, and recovery of sight to the blind, to set at liberty those who are oppressed; to proclaim the acceptable year of the Lord. (Luke 4:18–19)

As Jesus closed the book, the attention of every one was now firmly fixed upon Him. He then made the announcement that was destined to change the course of the world and send the demons of hell into a frenzy: "Today this scripture is fulfilled in your hearing" (Luke 4:21).

The news was out, heaven had spoken, the Son of God—the anointed one, the Messiah—had arrived and He had been anointed for a purpose to preach the Gospel. What Isaiah saw through the telescope of prophecy hundreds of years before had now come to pass.

When we consider the words "The Spirit of the Lord is upon Me," it is of utmost importance that we understand that the Holy Spirit (the anointing) came upon Jesus for a specific purpose—to preach the Gospel. The Holy Spirit always comes with purpose. He is the One who convicts the world of sin, of righteousness, and of judgment (John 16:10–11); He is always on mission. His purpose has never changed. He doesn't come to simply give us an experience but a purpose. Any individual or church who claims the infilling of the Holy Spirit will experience real purpose and will take seriously the real mission of the church "to make disciples" (Matt. 28:19–20).

Before disciples can be made, sinners have to be saved. Once there is genuine new birth by the Holy Spirit in response to the Gospel of Jesus Christ, the important issue then is for the new convert to become a disciple and follower of Jesus Christ.

In this book, I have chosen to deal with the subject of the Gospel of Jesus Christ rather than the making of disciples, although I have included a chapter on this. Having said that, what you will discover in reading through this book will be, I trust, a greater understanding of the power, privileges, and blessings that are freely given to those who embrace its truth by faith. Every follower and disciple of Jesus should understand these truths at the commencement of their walk with the Lord.

The Gospel Jesus announced was "good news," and it still is. In a world filled with bad news, thank God, we have some "good news." To the brokenhearted, oppressed, spiritually poor, and blind who have been captivated by sin and the devil, the Gospel offers deliverance and healing.

This is the Gospel we preach.

1

The Kingdom

Jesus sent out His disciples to heal the sick and proclaim "the kingdom of God is at hand" (Mark 1:15). This was as stated previously an alternative kingdom or rule as a contrast to the rule of sin and the power of Satan. The message of the Kingdom was the first message Jesus preached when He declared the Kingdom of God is at hand. The Gospel of the Kingdom not only runs through the Gospel accounts but also the book of the Acts of the Apostles.

Jesus made it clear that the Gospel of the Kingdom will be preached in all the world as a witness to all nations and *then* the end will come (Matt. 24:14). See also the continuation of the message of the Kingdom through the book of the Acts of the Apostles. In Jesus's last words on the Mount of Olives before ascending to His Father, He spoke of the Kingdom to His disciples (Acts 1:3; 8:12, 19:8, 20:25, 28:23, 28:31). Philip the evangelist preached this message in Samaria and Paul the Apostle even in his latter days when as a prisoner in Rome. He spent two years in his own rented house and received all who came to him, preaching the Kingdom of God.

Revealed in both the Old Testament and the New Testament is the truth of a literal kingdom which is to come, and a spiritual kingdom which operates in the hearts of those who turn to Christ.

The Jewish concept was to expect a literal Kingdom where the Messiah would rule, which we learn in the following passages:

The mountain of the Lord's house shall be established on the top of the mountains, and shall be exalted above the hills, and all nations shall flow to it … And the word of the Lord from Jerusalem. (Isa. 2:2–3)
For unto us a child is born, unto us a son is given, and the government shall be upon His shoulder. (Isa. 9:6–7)

His birth has been fulfilled, but the rest of the prophecy is yet to be fulfilled as we read in the book of Isaiah:

He shall strike the earth with the rod of His mouth. And with the breath of His lips He shall slay the wicked. (Isa. 11:4)
For the earth shall be full of the knowledge of the Lord, as the waters cover the sea. (Isa. 11:9)
For the Lord of Hosts will reign on Mount Zion and in Jerusalem, and before His elders gloriously. (Isa. 24:23)

This selection of passages taken from Isaiah's prophecy of a coming earthly kingdom bears witness to the prophetic writings of other OT prophets such as Daniel in Daniel 7:13–14), in Jeremiah 23:5, in Zechariah 14:9, and others.

In the NT, the book of Revelation, specifically Revelation 19:11–16, tells us "He will strike the nations and rule them with a rod of iron."

The Jewish hope was that the Messiah would come and deliver them from their oppressors. They had no concept of a suffering Messiah dying on a cross or of a spiritual Kingdom that would take root in the hearts of men. We have a wonderful account of the mother of James and John making a request for her two sons. James and John had left their fishing business to follow Jesus, but as Jesus is telling them of His coming suffering (Matt. 20:17–21), their mother makes her request.

It was a request that was centered on the coming Kingdom: "Grant that my two sons may sit one on your right hand and one on your left in your Kingdom." She has to be commended for boldness, but she was obviously biased toward her two sons. There are no limits to a mother's love! No wonder, when the other ten disciples heard this, they were displeased with James and John (Matt. 20:24).

The point I am making is simply that the earthly kingdom aspect of Christ's reign was uppermost in their thinking; the cross wasn't! Even Peter in Matthew 16 would receive a revelation that Jesus was the Son of the living God, but when Jesus spoke of suffering on the cross, Peter declared that this should not be so and was rebuked by Jesus.

Perhaps it was this Kingdom mentality that caused them to follow Him so readily and was the reason why they were willing to leave their fishing nets behind.

Jesus, on occasion, had to ask the crowds not to spread the news of some of the miracles because He knew they were ready to hail Him as king and this would have caused problems with the authorities of the day. There would come a time, of course, when they would cheer and cry Hosanna, saying, "Blessed is the King who comes in the name of the Lord!" But Jesus was always careful not simply to do what the Father told Him to do but also to be in step and time with His Father's perfect plan.

This was an understanding the disciples clearly had and were still thinking about when Jesus was about to ascend to His Father from the Mount of Olives: "Will You at this time restore the Kingdom to Israel?" (Acts 1:6).

After everything had transpired, the atrocities of crucifixion, the glorious resurrection, and all that had happened over the last forty days, including all the things Jesus had taught them during this period relative to His kingdom and purpose, they still asked the question, "Will You at this time restore the Kingdom to Israel?"

The plan and purpose of God was much bigger than that. The world had to be reached, and every nation had to hear the good news. The answer Jesus gave was to direct them to a time, just days away, when they would receive the Holy Spirit in power and then become His witnesses, eventually reaching out to the nations of the world.

I often wonder how Jesus must have felt when they asked that question. His agenda was much bigger than theirs. Thank God for His patience with all of us and for the continual revelation that He brings to us as we walk with Him.

Someone once said "If you want to make God laugh, tell Him your plans!"

The disciples were about to enter into much bigger plans than they had imagined, plans that would embrace the whole world, and they, in turn, would be accused of turning the world upside down with their message of the Kingdom.

The Kingdom message they were to spread would revolutionize the hearts of men, it would stir up hell, and it would cause riots and revivals. Families, towns, cities, and nations would be rocked by such a message; martyrs' blood would flow in order to spread this message. The disciples, who were obviously still in the school of learning, would soon come to realize that they needed Holy Spirit boldness and empowering; and that nothing short of hearts fully committed, with no limits to the sacrifice they would be called to make, was worthy of obeying the command of the resurrected Christ to "go into all the world and preach the Gospel and make disciples."

The message then was of a literal kingdom that would come to earth one day when Christ returned, and it also must be understood that through the new birth that Jesus spoke of in John 3, there is a spiritual kingdom. Paul teaches a translation from the power of darkness into the "Kingdom of God's dear Son" (Col. 1:13). There will be a literal rule of Christ one day on earth, and there is a spiritual rule in the hearts of those who have turned to Him and believed the Gospel.

The believer then looks for and anticipates the return of Jesus Christ and a literal Kingdom on earth and, at the same time, experiences the power of Christ's rule and Kingdom in power by and through His salvation and new life.

To a scribe who spoke with Jesus one day, Jesus said to him, "You are not far from the Kingdom of God." One step of faith and repentance and he could have stepped right into the most amazing experience of the rule of Christ in his heart.

The sad thing about this story that Mark records in Mark 12:28–34 is that we do not know if he took that step! Not far, one step away, is to remain lost and outside the Kingdom! The apostle Paul defines what the Kingdom of God is in Romans 14:17: "For the Kingdom of God is not eating and drinking, but righteousness and peace and joy in the Holy Spirit." How can anyone resist the greatest offer that heaven can make?

The disciples one day asked Jesus to teach them to pray. How often do people ask that question today? Sometimes it may be "Teach us to preach" or share our faith or a number of other requests *but* very rarely do we get asked to teach people to pray. The disciples had watched, listened, and taken note of His prayer life. They realized this was the secret to His authority and power. Jesus replied, "When you pray say …" We only really learn to pray when we start to pray. He went onto to give them some principles to prayer: "Our Father who art in heaven hallowed be your name 'Your Kingdom Come Your will be done in earth as it is in heaven …'" There it is—"Your Kingdom Come" (Luke 11).

My friend, it is coming and is here right now, just one step away.

This is the Gospel we preach.

2

Salvation

The word *salvation* both in the OT and the NT really denotes deliverance from almost any kind of evil. In the NT, it refers to the whole process by which man is delivered from all that interferes with the enjoyment of God's highest blessings (Zondervan Bible Dictionary). Paul uses this word *delivered* when teaching of the deliverance from the power of darkness and being conveyed into the Kingdom of God's dear Son. To be conveyed or translated into the Kingdom of God's Son—in other words, to come under Christ's rule and reign—there must be *deliverance*. This deliverance has to come from Jesus Himself: "He has delivered us." This has to be an intervention of God; salvation does not come through our own works or efforts (Eph. 2:9).

If the word *salvation* denotes "deliverance," then it follows there must be something that we need "delivering" from.

Sin is what disconnected Adam in the Garden of Eden. Adam disobeyed the command of God not to eat of the tree of the knowledge of good and evil. Adam's act of disobedience was rebellion, fully knowing the consequences of such an act. His wife, Eve, had already lost the glory of God and had become fallen in nature. Adam chose to fall to her level rather than remain in the high position of God's presence and favor. The devil had rebelled way back in eternity and suffered the consequences of being removed from the status of "anointed cherub," and through temptation, persuaded Adam to do the same (Ezekiel 28:11-19).

Sin separates—it binds, it blinds, and it deceives. But what actually is it? Paul teaches that it is transgression of the law (the Ten Commandments). The law was given as a schoolmaster or teacher to bring us to Christ (Galatians 3:24). The law condemns us, but Christ took our penalty when He died upon the cross.

Whenever I think of a schoolteacher, I vividly remember being about twelve years of age and sitting in class one day. The teacher asked us all a question, and one young lad raised his hand thinking he had the right answer. The answer he gave was clearly not right, and the teacher was so upset, he used the term "Good Heavens, boy, that's not right at all." The problem came when a young man called Brian Evans was asleep in class and suddenly woke up and heard the word *heavens*! When he said "Yes, sir," to the teacher in the form of a question, it was obvious he had been asleep.

In those days, if we stepped out of line, misbehaved, or were not listening, the teacher would punish us. It usually took the form of a whack by some large gym shoe on the backside! When Brian arose to take his punishment, the teacher reinforced the rule that when he was teaching, we must pay attention. I don't think Brian ever slept during class again!

The Ten Commandments reinforced the truth that we are sinners, we have all failed, and we are all under sin. But thanks be unto God, they were given as a schoolteacher to bring us to Christ. He is the one who offers us deliverance from sin's penalty.

Jesus also defined sin when He spoke of the Holy Spirit's work of convincing the world of sin as "the sin of unbelief." Too often we categorize sin with the things that we interpret as being "big sins" and "not so big sins." We think of murder, adultery theft, etc., when in actual fact Jesus clearly said that the sin that keeps us from God and would eternally damn our soul is the sin of unbelief (John 16:8–10). It is the penalty and power of sin from which we need deliverance.

The Gospel we preach offers salvation or deliverance from the penalty of sin. We live in a world where sin is often brushed over as a mistake or a failing, and to use the word sin is looked on as offensive. However, the Bible is clear on this issue and specifically tells us that we have all sinned and fallen short of God's glory. Repentance is a change of mind and is not a turning away from mistakes or simply failure but, rather, from sin—from everything that is offensive to God. The Gospel we preach must make clear what sin is. If there is no repentance, then there cannot possibly be any salvation.

There are far too many who think that salvation takes place by praying a simple prayer of asking Jesus into their heart, and repentance is never mentioned. Asking for forgiveness is not repentance either. Many ask for forgiveness and then go on to commit the same sin time and time again. The Gospel message demands repentance, a turning away from the things that have offended a holy God and a change of mind; it is a turnaround.

The story of the prodigal son illustrates this point. After wasting his inheritance on prostitutes and all the other sinful pursuits he could find, he decides to make his way home: "Father I have sinned against heaven and against you and I am no longer worthy to be called your son." (Luke 15). He didn't return, saying, "I have made a mistake" but "I have sinned against Heaven and you." The story has a great ending, of course. His Father throws a party and declares, "This my son was dead and is alive, was lost and is found." He had been dead as far as his relationship with his Father. Remember, when the son asked for his inheritance, he then went into a far country. He simply wanted his inheritance but didn't want His Father's presence! A Gospel that does not highlight sin and simply calls for people to believe in Jesus leaves them without the Father's presence, still spiritually dead in sin. Remember, "the wages of sin is death" (Rom. 6:23).

In the account of Peter's preaching in the house of Cornelius (Acts 10:18), we find these words after the Holy Spirit had fallen upon all who were in the house: "God has also granted to the Gentiles repentance unto life." There can be no real spiritual life if it is not first preceded by repentance. In Peter's preaching on the day of Pentecost (Acts 2:22–24), he nails sin to the door of the hearts of the men of Israel. "You have taken by lawless hands, have crucified, and put to death: whom God has raised up having loosed the pains of death, because it was not possible that He should be held by it." There was no mistake what their sin was—it wasn't a "mistake"; it was sin!

Notice what Acts 2:37 says: "When they heard this they were cut to the heart [conviction of sin] and asked what they could do." The answer came back: "Repent and be baptized." In the NT, the Gospel they preached demanded repentance, and for that to take place sin had to be exposed. Once there is repentance repented, the good news of the Gospel we preach is that there is not only forgiveness but salvation, which brings a spiritual new birth (John 3) and with it the life of God.

Eternal life is often simply taken as meaning "life eternal" in heaven, but it also means the life of the Eternal God. What a miracle that the "zoe" God kind of life is given to us. The apostle John writes, "He who has the Son has life and he that does not have the Son does not have life" (1 John 5:12). God had declared to Adam in the Garden of Eden that if he were to eat of the tree of the knowledge of good and evil, in that day he would die. Adam died spiritually that day—his spirit, the eternal part of him, was separated from God. The one who had been created to have fellowship and relationship with the Father was now separated by sin and spiritual death.

Through the shed blood of Jesus as He died upon the cross and took our penalty (the wages of sin is death), He now offers restoration to what Adam lost—life, the life of God and relationship with our Creator. The very purpose and reason for God giving us eternal life is that we may know Him as the only true God and Jesus Christ whom He has sent (John 17:3). Paul declares, "Christ died for our sins" (1 Cor. 15:3); and when He did, He paid the penalty of sin. The Gospel we preach offers salvation from the penalty of sin and the power of sin. Salvation or deliverance also deals with the power of sin.

When Paul wrote to the Ephesian church (Eph. 2), he declares that "they were once dead in trespasses and sins, but had been made alive" (Eph. 2:1) and in Eph. 2:2 describes their former way of life under the dictatorship of "the prince of the power of the air" (devil). They followed their own lusts and desires of their darkened minds and sinful nature. But Paul had good news—a God who is rich in mercy had intervened (Eph. 2:4).

All this happened because Paul had the passion and courage to go to the great city of Ephesus and preach the Gospel. He had accompanying signs and wonders (Acts 19) and a great revival as well as much persecution. Notice what Paul actually says in Ephesians 2:2–3: "You once walked according to the course of this world" and "among whom also we all 'once' conducted ourselves in the lusts of the flesh fulfilling the desires of the flesh and of the mind." What they did once or during the years of not knowing God's salvation, they now no longer did.

The Gospel we preach delivers from the power of sin. The new nature, of course, has to be spiritually fed upon God's Word. We have to learn to walk in the Spirit (or walk with the Lord, which is an ongoing, maturing experience); and as we do, the things that once dominated our lives and held us captive under their sway are broken. The power of sin should not dominate us (Rom. 6:14).

Although sin should not be the master of our lives and dominate our actions, we also must recognize that we have not been delivered from the presence of sin. Paul exhorts in Romans 6:12, "Do not let sin reign in your mortal body that you should obey it in its lusts." Thank God one day we will see the Lord and be with Him and full salvation will be complete. John declares in 1 John 3:1–3, "When we see Him we shall be like Him for we will see Him as He is." On that day, we will be delivered from the presence of sin.

In the book of Daniel, we find the story of Daniel and his three companions who were given the name of Shadrach, Meshach, and Abednego. (We would often tell the children in Sunday school the best way to remember their name was by "my shack," "your shack," and a "bungalow.") They were all being trained to wait upon the King Nebuchadnezzar. They had been taken captive from Judah, had tracked the one thousand miles to Babylon, and had been chosen for this special position. The king had a dream, and only Daniel could interpret it. He described the dream to the king of a great image.

The king was well pleased with Daniel and promoted him. He then ordered a great image to be made, and the decree was issued that as music was played in symphony that everyone was to bow down and worship the image. Daniel's three companions refused. The king heard the news and was outraged. He ordered them to be thrown into the fiery furnace. He was so mad that he had it heated up seven times hotter than usual. The three were fully clothed and bound hand and foot. As they were thrown into furnace, the soldiers that threw them in were burned with the flames and killed. Nebuchadnezzar eventually looked into the furnace and, to his utter shock, saw four men walking in the flames. He describes the fourth man as like the "Son of God." He ordered them to come out; and as they did, there was no burnt clothes and not a hair of their head was singed. It was then that Nebuchadnezzar made a tremendous, prophetic statement that would be true for all eternity: "There is no other God who can deliver like this" (Dan. 3:29).

How true that is, delivered from the power of darkness, translated into the Kingdom of His dear Son, delivered from the penalty and power of sin, and delivered from future judgment in an eternal hell? Every one of us should echo these words: "There is no other God who can deliver like this."

The gospel we preach definitely is Good News.

3

Christ and Cross Centered

Paul, when writing to the Corinthian church, declared,

> For Christ did not send me to baptize, but to preach the gospel, not with wisdom of words, lest the cross of Christ should be made of no effect. For the message of the cross is foolishness to those who are perishing, but to us who are being saved it is the power of God. (1 Cor. 1:17–18)

Throughout the OT, there are many types and shadows of the cross. To cast a shadow, you need an object and light. I remember as a boy walking through our village on dark winter nights being unafraid. The reason was, my dad was just a few yards behind; and as long as I could see his shadow cast by the street light, I knew I was safe. I like to imagine God the Father in His blazing and awesome glory shining upon His Beloved Son way back in eternity. As He did, He cast shadows through all the OT period. The sacrifices Israel was commanded to bring to the altar in the tabernacle courtyard pointed to the One great sacrifice who was coming. The smiting of the rock in the wilderness by Moses, as Israel thirsted for water spoke of the smiting of Christ at Calvary, meant from Him would come living water—the kind of water that He promised the woman of Samaria in John 4 that if she would drink, she would never thirst again.

There are so many, it would take too long to mention them all; but I will draw your attention particularly to two the first one being the offering up of Isaac by Abraham his father on Mount Moriah (Genesis 22). The whole story of Abraham and Sarah is a story of the triumph of faith. It is God choosing a man and promising to make from him a great nation.

Revelation came to Abraham in stages. It was first of a call to go to a land that God would show him as he started out on the journey. It is a story of faith and patience. Most of us don't take too easily to the patience part; we want things to happen immediately, if at all possible. But Abraham had to learn that it would be through faith and patience he and Sarah would inherit the promises.

It is also amazing how many chapters of the book of Genesis are devoted to his incredible story from chapter 11 through to chapter 25, and yet just a few chapters deal with creation! God takes great delight in the transformation of men and women. The promise of a child that would be his heir, yet everything in the natural pointed to this being impossible. Sarah could not conceive and every passing year seemed to underline the impossibility of this promise ever being fulfilled. In the process of building Abraham's faith, God had to show him that the supernatural transcends the natural. In Genesis 15, God takes Abraham outside and shows him the stars, "So shall your descendants be" (Gen. 15:5).

The Lord was seeking to implant a vision into Abraham's mind. Before we can receive the promise, we have to see it. Sometimes, we have to step outside our normal day-to-day routine and it can be at such times we see things more clearly. I have often found this to be the case when I have been away from pastoral duties and ministering in another country that God has opened my eyes to greater possibilities and challenged me toward change.

In the same chapter, Genesis 15, Abraham falls into a deep sleep; and once again, God confirms His covenant. Even with these confirmations, everything in the natural looked bleak: "Sarai, Abram's wife, had borne him no children. And she had an Egyptian maidservant whose name was Hagar" (Gen. 16:1). Natural reasoning dominated their thinking, and Sarai encouraged Abram to have a relationship with the maid. The result was that Ishmael was born.

The consequences were, friction between the two women and, eventually, Hagar had to leave. Abraham had to stand and watch as she walked away with his son into the desert! In Genesis 17, Abram had reached the ripe old age of ninety-nine years; and despite what had previously happened, the Lord announces Himself as "*I am Almighty God,*" [my italics] walk before Me and be blameless."

God's grace and patience is amazing. What greater encouragement to faith! When everything seems utterly impossible, there is still God who is "the Almighty." A dead womb and a frail body were the facts and circumstances that stood in the way of the promise being fulfilled, but that was simply in the natural realm. Now the God who dwells in the eternal, supernatural realm has announced Himself as "the Almighty," and a dead womb and frail body must respond to the One who spoke worlds into being!

Twenty five years waiting for a promise and each year made it seem more impossible, but God was bringing Abraham to a place of faith. He had heard the word of the Lord, seen the stars, a deep sleep had brought him a vision of the covenant keeping God. He had heard and he had seen, and now he has to speak. God changed his name from Abram to Abraham ("father of a multitude") and Sarai to Sarah ("princess") (Gen. 17). Seeing and hearing were not enough; they now had to speak and confess the promise. It is interesting to note that in Genesis 17:5, when God informed Abram of his name change, He then said to him, "For I have made you a father of many nations." This is the past tense! With God, this had already happened! He just needed Abraham to activate it by faith.

Paul, in Romans 4:17–21, tells us that Abraham's faith grew so much so that he did not consider his own body already dead and the deadness of Sarah's womb! He did not waver in faith but gave glory to God and became fully convinced that what He had promised He was able to perform. Fully convinced! Doubt had gone, even though he and Sarah had laughed at such a thought, and there is this wonderful verse in the book of Genesis, we read:

> And the Lord visited Sarah's as he had said and the Lord did for Sarah as he had spoken. For Sarah conceived and bore Abraham a son in his old age. (Gen. 21:1–2)

When we spend time with each other, the term *we've been visiting* is often used. When God "visits," things change and miracles happen! The very name *Isaac* means "laughter." What a joy it was to this aged couple's heart, what love and devotion they must have given him! Every day, as they looked at him, they were reminded of the miracle promise of God. Words could never describe the joy he brought to their hearts.

It was years later, when Isaac was a young man, that the "test" came, one of the greatest types of Calvary was enacted. God said to Abraham, "Take your son 'your only son Isaac whom you love and go to the land of Moriah, and offer him there as a burnt offering on one of the mountains which I shall tell you" (Gen. 22:2). Abraham, Isaac, and two servants journeyed for three days until Abraham saw the place in the distance where he was to offer up his son. Abraham leaves the servants behind, telling them that he and Isaac would go and worship and would return. Wood, fire, a knife, and, of course, a sacrifice!

Isaac saw all these things but asked where the sacrifice was. We have the wonderful inspiration of scripture recorded in verse 8: "My son God will provide for Himself the lamb for a burnt offering." The sacrifice at Calvary was first "for God Himself." The holiness and judgment of God had to be satisfied before God could offer the world His salvation. We hear so much of the love and grace of God but little of His judgment and holiness in modern preaching. The God of the Bible is governed by His character, and He does not change. He is a God of holiness and demands judgment on sin. He is a God who is Truth and He cannot lie. He is a God of love and will never turn away the repentant sinner. He is a God who never changes—perfection does not need to change.

The cross, as Isaiah describes in Isaiah 53, portrays Christ taking the judgment of sin upon Himself and becoming sin for us. Abraham takes his "only son" (notice again the inspiration of Scripture); God was not recognizing Ishmael who had been born to Hagar. The son of promise, Isaac, is his only son. He was the type of the "only begotten Son that God gave" (John 3:16).

I cannot describe the tension of this moment as Abraham looked down at his son, Isaac, bound to the altar. His mind must have rushed through all the years of waiting, the tests and trials along the way, the joy of holding his son in his arms, and the times that he and Sarah had both lifted their hearts toward heaven in praise of a God who keeps His promises. Now, he held a knife, and his son's chest was only inches away. He raised his hand to plunge the knife into Isaac's chest, and the Angel of the Lord called to him. "Do not lay your hand upon your son or do anything to him, now I know that you fear God, since you have not withheld your son, your only son, from me" (Gen. 22:12).

Abraham looks around and behind him was a ram caught in the thicket. The lamb previously promised was obviously referring to the Lamb of God who would come into the world as a sacrifice for sin.

I have often wondered how long the ram was there! Maybe in the supernatural realm, God had hidden it from Abraham's eyes until he needed to see it. Abraham gave a name to that place and called it *Jehovah Jireh*—"the Lord will provide"; "in the mount of the Lord it shall be provided." We often hear this name quoted referring to God providing, and it is usually in the context of material provision. But we need to be reminded that the greatest provision God ever made was when His only begotten Son died on the mount called Calvary. Hundreds of years later, Jesus said of Abraham, "Your Father Abraham rejoiced to see My day and he saw it and was glad" (John 8:56). On Mount Moriah, Abraham saw the day of the Lord. He saw what was coming and rejoiced.

This was a test, not a temptation. When God tests us, it is in order to bring out what we have learned, very similar to the tests we do at school or college. If you pass the test, you move on to the next level. Abraham moved up another level of faith as he passed the test; and at the same time, through his obedience, he received further revelation—he saw Christ's day. A temptation is different from a test. A temptation is designed to cause us to fail. The Lord does not tempt us, but He will test us. The devil will throw temptation our way in order for us to fail. Abraham and Isaac are one of the greatest types and shadows in the OT.

The Lord Jesus gave the two disciples a Bible study as they walked along the road to Emmaeus. Not knowing that He was the resurrected Christ, as they listened, their hearts burned within them (Luke 24:27). Beginning with Moses and all the prophets, Jesus expounded the scriptures concerning Himself to them. What a Bible study that must have been as He, the greatest teacher of all, opened up the scriptures and explained to them all the types and shadows of His suffering, resurrection, and glory.

Paul, when writing to the Corinthian church, declared his primary message was to preach Christ and Him crucified (1 Cor. 2:2). The message of the cross may still seem foolishness to many, but this is the Gospel that we preach. One man paid the ultimate price for the sins of the world—one man, the man Christ Jesus, who humbled Himself to take upon Himself human nature and dwell among us, the Son of the living God who walked this world and, yet without sin, became the perfect, spotless sacrifice, fulfilling all OT types and shadows when He died upon the cross. Divine blood flowed from His wounds, blood that cried out to a dying world, "There is forgiveness, salvation, a way of escape, a new life if you will believe."

"It is finished" was His cry from the cross, and everything was complete. It was like the Great Artist and Creator of the universe had put the last stroke of his brush to the masterpiece and then it was complete. The wisdom of God had created a way for all, no matter what the color of their skin, their background, upbringing, and even the enormity of their sin, it would not be by worldly wisdom or intellectual ability that men would discover salvation. It would be by gazing at the cross, by looking and seeing with the eyes of faith. This was indeed the master plan of God.

The second type I want to draw your attention to is the 'lifting up of the serpent in the wilderness'. A certain Pharisee by the name of Nicodemus came to Jesus one night, recognizing He must be someone special because of the miracles He did (John 3). Jesus told Nicodemus that he must be born again or he would not even see the Kingdom of God. This term had never been used before in a spiritual sense, and Nicodemus couldn't understand how such a thing could ever be possible. "Can a man enter a second time into his mother's womb and be born?" it says so in John 3:4.

We may smile at such a question, but at this point, it was all new to Nicodemus. It is interesting to consider Jesus's answer: "As Moses lifted up the serpent in the wilderness even so must the Son of man be lifted up, that whoever believes in Him should not perish but have everlasting life" (John 3:14). The account of the lifting up of the serpent is found in Numbers 21. Israel was in the wilderness on their journey toward the promised land and once again became discouraged and complained against their leader, Moses. "Why have you brought us up out of Egypt to die in the wilderness for there is no food and no water and our soul loathes this worthless bread" (Num. 21:5).

The reader must understand that prior to this complaint, they had continually had the presence of God with them—a cloud by day and a pillar of fire by night. They had seen miraculous provision as they had escaped from Egypt and the Red Sea had parted. They had crossed on dry ground, and the pursuing army of Egyptians had been drowned as they tried to overtake them. Moses had, on two occasions, struck the rock and water had gushed forth. Although on the second time, he was told only to speak to the rock and not to strike it. The Hebrew word for rock on the second occasion is "elevated one," which speaks of the ascended Christ after Calvary.

To smite this rock was to spoil the type. Jesus cannot be crucified a second time. He died "once and for all." Israel also had the opportunity of crossing Jordan with the promises of God that He would fight for them against all enemies, but fear had gripped the majority. Democracy ruled; and when democracy rules over the will of God, there are consequences.

Fiery serpents were sent among the tribes of Israel, and every person bitten died. Moses intercedes for the nation, and the word of the Lord was that he should make a replica snake out of brass and place it high upon a pole. The command to Israel was, if they were bitten and had the sentence of death upon them, they must look at the serpent on the pole and they would live.

This is the story that Jesus related to Nicodemus in answer to his question as to how a man could be born again: "As Moses lifted up the serpent in the wilderness even so must the son of man be lifted up that whoever believes in Him should not perish but have eternal life" (John 3:14–15). It was crystal-clear—the new birth would take place in a person's heart if they dare to look at the cross. It was only people who realized the sentence of death was upon them that looked at the serpent!

Today, it is the same. It is the sinner who recognizes he has no hope outside Jesus's sacrifice upon the cross. Whoever, metaphorically, falls at the foot of the blood-stained cross and lifts his eyes to the mangled, tortured, pain-racked body of Jesus Christ and sees the blood that was shed for the sins of the world becomes a part of the saving miracle. Just one look, the look of faith and repentance, and then deliverance takes place. This is the Gospel we preach.

Psalm 85:10–11 declares, "Mercy and truth have met together, righteousness and peace have kissed each other." At the cross, it is the great meeting place. God's mercy and truth meet together. The truth standing alone condemns, us but mercy meets it. Similarly, John writes, "And the Word became flesh and dwelt among us and we beheld His glory as of the only begotten of the Father full of grace and truth" (John 1:14).

Grace—thank God—also meets with truth; truth alone would slay us, but grace grants us undeserved favor. Jesus delivered the Truth because He is the Truth, but He is also full of grace. The Gospel we preach must declare the truth along with the grace of God.

Similarly, "righteousness and peace" have kissed each other. The One who is righteous and without sin offers peace to the unrighteous, to undeserving sinners. When we gaze at the cross, God's wisdom, holiness, righteousness, grace, mercy, truth, peace, judgment, wrath, compassion, and forgiveness all meet at Calvary. This is God's master plan that Jesus gave Himself willingly in order to fulfill and offer us His salvation and a radical experience which is called being "born again."

The cross may offend some, but it will also convict and convert. It will cause reactions as the souls of men wrestle with truth, and the powers of hell do all they can to distract and deceive. Having said that, there is a wonderful magnetism of the cross. It may take men through the wrestling of conscience and it will strike at the heart of their sin and fears, but its power is undiminished. It is still drawing men and women right across our world into salvation, peace, and the joy of knowing the living God.

We preach Christ crucified. This is the Gospel we preach.

4

A New Creation

The Bible says, "Therefore if anyone is in Christ, he is a new creation: old things have passed away, behold all things have become new" (2 Cor. 5:17). The apostle Peter wrote 'grace and peace be multiplied to you in the knowledge of God and of Jesus our Lord as His divine power has given to us all things that pertain to life and godliness through the knowledge of Him who called us by glory and virtue, by which we have been given great and precious promises, that through these you may be partakers of the divine nature, having escaped the corruption that is in the world through lust. 2 Peter 1:2-4

The Message (paraphrased edition) says 'we were given absolutely terrific promises to pass onto you, your tickets to participation in the life of God after you turned your back on a world corrupted by sin'.

The question must be asked 'how can we become partakers of the divine nature or participants in the life of God? The answer is by 'being born again not of corruptible seed but incorruptible, through the life of God which lives and abides forever...' 1Peter1:23

This is the miracle the new nature the divine nature is deposited within the believer which is not a make-over of the old but a new nature.

In 2 Corinthians 5:17, Paul explains the believer's position in Christ—that is, of being "a new creation." The understanding of this truth is vital. Paul uses the term *in Christ*, which is our positional status. It has been well said that "what we believe determines the way we behave." The expositions that Paul and the other NT writers give us are to make us aware of our new position in Christ; and from this, they further exhort believers to a new lifestyle that should accompany those who name the name of Christ. Paul's prayer is that the

> eyes of our understanding should be enlightened that we may *know* [my italics] what is the hope of His calling ... Our understanding, the revelation of what He has done for us ... what we have been brought into, will lead to a new lifestyle. (Eph. 1:17–23)

In Ephesians 2, after the description of what these believers used to be like prior to conversion, he leads them through this second chapter to tell them of their new position (Eph. 2:6) of being raised up together and made to sit in heavenly places in Christ Jesus.

Knowing our position changes the way we conduct our lives and leads to progress in our walk of faith with the Lord.

Dr. Martin Lloyd Jones writes, "We must differentiate between what is our position as a fact and our experience." By "position," Lloyd Jones means that a Christian is as a new man.

The new creation is the new nature of Christ formed in the believer; yet at the same time, there is still the old nature. The new nature is sinless, which does not mean that the believer never sins. The apostle John tells us that "he that says he has no sin deceives himself and the truth is not in him" (1 John 1:8). At first glance, some of these scriptures seem to be contradictory. The new nature is sinless and the believer becomes a new creation with the power of new life. It is from this position that God views the believer. We also know that from experience we can still struggle with sin because the believer has a choice—the choice is which nature will the believer allow to dominate their thinking and behavior!

THE GOSPEL WE PREACH

In Romans 6, Paul says we died to sin (Rom. 6:2) and then asks the question, *How shall we who died to sin live any longer in it?* In Romans 6:3, he says we were baptized into His death. In Romans 6:6, it says, "Knowing that our old man was crucified with Him that the body of sin might be done away with, that we should no longer be slaves to sin." Our "old man" is referring to our old position before salvation.

Having said all that, Paul then says that we are to "reckon" ourselves to be dead indeed to sin but alive to God in Christ Jesus our Lord (Rom. 6:11). The word *reckon* means that we are to put into experience and live out what our position in Christ is. If, automatically, we no longer struggled with the flesh (or "self" life), then there would not be the exhortations for us to "put on the new man" and "to reckon ourselves to be dead to sin."

When writing to the Galatian church (Gal. 5), Paul exhorts believers to "walk in the Spirit and they would not fulfill the lusts of the flesh" (Gal. 5:16). Is it possible for a believer to fulfill lusts of the flesh? Absolutely. It comes down to choices as to which nature we allow to dominate. The spiritual life in Christ must be allowed to go on to perfection or maturity as we fellowship with the Lord and learn to walk by faith. When Paul warned of the last days that some will not endure sound doctrine but will simply want their ears tickling (2 Tim. 4:3), this should challenge every one of us. Every preacher of the Gospel needs to be aware of this solemn warning and make sure we preach the Gospel that offers a new creation, a brand-new position with the power of the Holy Spirit to live it out.

When the apostle Paul wrote to the churches in the NT, he constantly used the term *in Christ* when referring to believers. The believer is eternally united with Christ and is described as having been buried with Him (baptism) and raised in newness of life, also seated with Him in the heavenly places, and is a joint heir with Him and heir of the Father (Rom. 8:17). As Paul Bilheimer says in his book *Destined for the Throne*, "We are exalted next of kin to the trinity." There is no greater privilege! Our position before being born again is that of "being inn Adam," so everything he represented was ours too. Unfortunately, he sinned, died spiritually, and lost connection with God; and we were in Adam!

Paul teaches in 2 Corinthians 5:14–15, "If one died for all [Christ] then all died. And He died for all that those who live should no longer live for themselves but for Him who died for them and rose again." This is the truth that is missed by millions who believe that salvation is on the basis of their good works. If a person is spiritually dead, the first thing they need is a spiritual resurrection! So-called good works can never achieve this. It can only take place by the "quickening or making alive by the Holy Spirit" through repentance and faith.

Through this new position and new life in Christ, Paul declares in Romans 6:14 that "sin will not have dominion over you." As we have previously stated, the believer is not free from sin as long as the old nature exists. What Paul is teaching is that sin will not have dominion over the believer as long as he or she reckons themselves to be dead to sin. Spiritual success is ours through the salvation and new life that is imparted to us. Ours is the choice as to what we allow to dominate our lives.

The believer must see this new position and understand the reality of the new birth. As newborn babes, Peter exhorts the believers to desire the sincere milk of the Word of God that they may grow in Christ (1 Pet. 2:2). The natural and the spiritual are opposites. If a believer decides to fast for several days, the chances are, they will feel hungry! If, as a believer, we start to neglect the reading and studying of the Bible along with prayer and fellowship with God's people, the opposite takes place—we start to lose desire for God. The natural or old nature is still within us, but thank God for the miracle life of Christ that is imparted to us that make us a new creation.

Consider this passage: "Old things pass away and all things become new" (2 Cor. 5:17). Everything associated with "spiritual death" passes away; we enter into a new life and a walk of faith. New priorities become ours; the old things that once consumed us like the pleasures of sin pass away.

To the believers who had come out of the legalities of Judaism, into faith in Christ, everything was different. The apostle Paul, who once was a Pharisee bent on destroying the church of Christ, declared in Philippians 3:13, "I am forgetting those things which are behind and pressing forth to those things which are ahead." Paul was captivated by a desire and passion to know Christ intimately. He was taken up by the new revelation of the cross the resurrection and the transformation Jesus brings into the human heart.

The apostle Peter said,

> For we have spent enough of our past lifetime in doing the will of the Gentiles when we walked in lewdness, lusts, drunkenness, revelries, drinking parties and abominable idolatries. In regard to these they think it strange that you do not run with them in the same flood of dissipation, speaking evil of you. (1 Pet. 4:3–4)

We don't run after those things anymore. We have new things that far excel the old lifestyle. Live for the new—it's a new life, new hope, and a new kingdom.

The story is told of an eagle's egg that was stolen from the nest. It was taken to a farm and placed in among the chicken eggs that had newly been laid. In due time, all the eggs hatched. Inside one of them was a little eaglet. The problem was that, as he grew, he didn't look like a chicken but he thought he was a chicken. He behaved like a chicken and clucked like a chicken. He grew to be much bigger than all the other chickens. His wingspan was much wider, but he walked around the farmyard, convinced he was a chicken.

The day came when an eagle flew over the farmyard, and the young eaglet looked up and asked the chicken next to him, "What is that?" The chicken replied, "That's an eagle, but you can never do that because you are a chicken." So off they walked together, clucking away, and the eaglet that grew into a large eagle never left the farmyard. He never did soar to the heights he was created for. His feet never left the ground because he thought he was a chicken!

As believers, we must know the truth of who we are in Christ and go on to be transformed by the renewing of our mind. We were never created to be earthbound!

When Lazarus was raised from the dead in John 11, he had been in the tomb for four days. Jesus waited, having received the news that his friend Lazarus was sick. He was intent on His disciples seeing the glory of God in the miracle of resurrection. Also at that time, the Jews had this idea or belief that the soul of a dead person would linger somewhere in the atmosphere for a period of three days before actually passing into eternity. Maybe that is another reason why Jesus waited for four days! Perhaps He wanted the people to understand that when He declared Himself to be the "resurrection and the life," they would actually believe it. I think this is one of the most amazing stories in the NT.

Imagine the heartbreak of the two sisters, Mary and Martha, they had just watched their brother fall sick and, within days, had died. The question *Where is Jesus when we really need Him?* was obviously on their minds. Too often, we are guilty of doubting and not understanding what the Lord is doing when we hit a crisis. I think frustration was at a fever pitch when Martha finally sees Jesus coming, but now it's too late. Or was it? She knew He worked miracles, testimony after testimony had confirmed this, but in her eyes, all that grief and heartbreak could have been avoided. "Lord if you had been here, my brother would not have died," she says in John 11:21. "But even now I know that whatever you ask of God, God will give you," she adds in John 11:22. What a statement, "Even now." We should always remember, it is never too late for God to step into the situation and bring about a miracle. You may be left wondering, *How can things change? Can this sickness be healed? Can this marriage be saved? This prodigal restored?*

There are so many situations that we face in this fallen world, but there is always an "even now" waiting for you. Martha went on to state her unfailing faith in the great resurrection by saying "I know that he will rise again in the resurrection at the last day" (John 11:24). Then Jesus made the statement that said it all: "I am the resurrection and the life, He who believes in Me, though he may die, he shall live. And whoever lives and believes in Me shall never die. Do you believe this?" (John 11:25–26). In which Martha replied, "Yes, Lord I believe You are the Christ the son of the living God, who is come into the world" (John 11:27).

Jesus made it abundantly clear that *resurrection* is not just a date in God's calendar but *the resurrection* is none other than Jesus Himself! With tear-stained cheeks, Martha was actually looking at "the Resurrection and the Life." The rest was a foregone conclusion. Lazarus would experience "resurrection" within moments of that conversation.

When they loosed Lazarus from his grave clothes and set him free, we never read that he periodically went back into the tomb for a day or two! I remember one preacher said jokingly, "If I knew the place where I was going to die, I would stay away from that place as long as I live."

The tomb represented death. Why would Lazarus ever think of spending time in the place that he had been delivered from? If you have experienced the new life and salvation of Christ, never contemplate going back to the old way of life. it smells of death.

The new life is better than the old; the new creation is better than the old creation.

"If any man is in Christ" means we all have a choice to make.

The Gospel we preach offers a new creation.

5

The Holy Spirit Is Our Guarantee

As mentioned earlier in the book, the new birth comes as a result of the work of the Holy Spirit; the believer is "born again of the Spirit."

Paul teaches in Romans 8:9, "Now, if anyone does not have the Spirit of Christ he is not His" which is also expressed in Romans 8:11:

> But if the Spirit of Him who raised Jesus from the dead dwells in you, He who raised Jesus from the dead will also give life to your mortal bodies through His Spirit that dwells in you.

In the same chapter, Romans 8:15–16 states,

> For you did not receive the spirit of bondage again to fear but you received the Spirit of adoption by whom we cry "Abba Father." The Spirit Himself bears witness with our spirit that we are the children of God.

To the Ephesian believers, he writes of the Holy Spirit that He is our guarantee:

> Having believed you were sealed with the Holy Spirit of promise, who is the guarantee of our inheritance

until the redemption of the purchased possession to the
praise of His glory. (Eph. 1:13–14)

Every believer has a guarantee—it is the Holy Spirit. This guarantee holds fast until the "redemption of the purchased possession." The death of Christ paid a price that covers our spirit, soul, and body. At His appearing believers, who are alive at that moment, will be changed and their mortal bodies will put on immortality. Those who have died in Christ will also have a new body at that moment; the corruptible body will put on incorruption (1 Cor. 15). Until that time comes, we are blessed with a guarantee.

The Holy Spirit is also called the Spirit of adoption; He enters our spirit at the new birth and witnesses with our spirit that we are children of God. Our response is to cry "Abba Father." We know we have a guarantee through the Word of God and by the Holy Spirit's witness within.

It was the spirit of Adam that died or was disconnected from God when he sinned. The entrance of the Holy Spirit into our spirit brings spiritual resurrection to those who were once dead in sin (Eph. 2:1).

The three parts of our makeup are often not fully understood. Before the new birth, we operated with two parts—body and soul. The body is obviously our physical being, the soul is our will and emotions, and our spirit is that part of us that God created to be receptive to His voice and presence.

"The spirit of man is the candle of the Lord, searching all the inner depths of his heart," the passage in Proverbs 20:27 says. God seeks to bring us revelation and commune with us in our spirit as we learn to listen to His whispers. It is into our spirit that the Holy Spirit comes to bring us the witness and assurance that we are "born of God."

I have often heard people say "I think God is trying to speak to me." The truth is, God speaks—He doesn't have to try—and it is we who have to learn to listen to the still, small voice in our spirit. In the midst of Jesus's temptation, when Satan tempted Him to turn stones into bread, His answer was, "Man shall not live by bread alone but by every word that proceeds from the mouth of God" (Matt. 4:4). The word *proceeds* is present tense—that is, God is speaking.

Our problem is that, before salvation, our soul and emotions dominated the way we felt; and this was generally based on what our circumstances were. The believer receives new life by the Holy Spirit; He comes to dwell in our spirit. But for real transformation to take place, the soul must be renewed. It can no longer be in the driving seat of our lives; otherwise, we will always be prone to mood swings, depending on circumstances as to whether we are filled with joy or depression.

Paul teaches that the mind (soul) must be renewed (Rom. 12:1–3). The soul and mind worked independently of our spirit prior to salvation, but afterward, it must become subservient to the spirit. If this does not take place, the life of God within our spirit is stifled; and the treasure that we have in our earthen vessels is hidden and dominated by an unrenewed mind.

Years ago, we used to have cassette recorders; and the small cassette tape was placed in the recorder, and when the record button was pressed, the tape would capture the sounds being recorded. Throughout our lives, in our subconscious, we have recorded many things—some good and some not so good. The thoughts of failure and hurts and the words that have been spoken over us accumulate over the years; and without realizing, they affect our behavior and outlook on life. It was easy, of course, to erase the cassette tape and wipe it clean so that something new could be recorded. The process of renewing our mind or soul takes time, and it is a process that happens as the Word of God washes our minds clean.

When a certain preacher was exhorting the congregation to memorize verses of scripture, someone interrupted him and told him that he had difficulty in remembering verses and even sermons. The person then went to say that he felt he was like a bucket that had holes in it and that he had difficulty retaining what was taught. The preacher answered by telling him that even if there are holes in a bucket and water is continually poured in, the bucket may not retain the water but it would definitely be clean!

As we begin to discover who we are in Christ, our soul begins to prosper because it becomes restored and clean from the pollutions of wrong thinking that have accumulated over the years. We are exhorted to receive with meekness the Word of God which is able to "save" our souls (James 1:21). James is obviously writing to believers and encouraging them to be doers of the Word. We must not make the mistake of thinking that every time this word *save* is used, it is referring to salvation. The word *save* in this verse refers to "restoration." The upholsterer may receive an old armchair—tattered, torn, and worn—but after he has worked on it, the armchair looks brand-new, i.e., restored. The psalmist David said, "He restores my soul" (Ps. 23).

Spiritual prosperity comes when our soul prospers or is restored and no longer assumes the driving seat of our lives but allows the Spirit to lead. Remember this passage: "Beloved I pray that you may prosper and be in health, just as your soul prospers" (3 John 1:2).

For the perfume to come forth from the alabaster box, the box had to be broken (Matt. 26:7). All the negative thoughts, pride, self-importance, wrong thinking, and all the old conditioning of past hurts abuse and all the scars the old life have accumulated must be dealt with. The hurts and abuse must come under God's healing balm, the pride and self-importance must be brought to the cross, and the negative thoughts must be transformed. In God's dealings with us, He often allows situations that refine us, that bring to the surface things that we may never have noticed ourselves—hidden fears, insecurities, and low self-esteem, for example.

In the midst of some of life's storms and valleys, we are forced to throw ourselves upon God for His help. The psalmist said, "In my distress the Lord enlarged me" (Ps. 118:5). As we understand God's dealings and allow Him to renew and change us, the treasure of the life of God flows through us. It is wonderful to be in the presence of such perfume—faith rises, downcast spirits are encouraged and refreshed, lives are touched and changed. The Holy Spirit can do more in moments than we can do in a lifetime. We must not allow His life to be stifled; rather, let it become a river bringing life to all it touches.

The apostle Paul declared that he served God with his spirit in the Gospel of Christ (Rom. 1:8). Circumstances, trials, persecutions, and beatings did not deter him; he didn't serve from his soul (emotions) but his spirit. One more last thought to consider on this subject is this: "Mary said 'My soul magnifies the Lord, and my spirit has rejoiced in God my Savior'" (Luke 1:46–47). Her soul magnified the Lord because her spirit had rejoiced in God her Savior. When our spirit is in the driving seat, our soul will follow!

Smith Wigglesworth used to say, "When people ask me how Mr. Wigglesworth is, I tell them I never ask how he is, I tell him how he is!"

The Holy Spirit is the Spirit of Life. However we may interpret Romans 7, whether this is Paul referring back to preconversion days and describing his struggle to please God or whether it is the struggle of the believer with the old nature dominating the new, the answer is found in Romans 8.

We are introduced to "the law of the Spirit of life" in Christ Jesus. This law sets us free from the old law of sin and death. If we choose to "walk according to the Spirit," we walk in victory (Rom. 8:4). God has made provision for every one of us to be free to live as victors and not victims. The Gospel of Jesus Christ offers spiritual resurrection, new life, and the Holy Spirit of God residing in our spirit to bring us into freedom from the struggles of sin.

It is this relationship and experience whereby we cry "Abba Father" (Rom. 8:15) that fills our hearts with the assurance of eternal life, and we know of a certainty that we are children of God. Not only children of God but heirs of God and joint heirs with Jesus Christ (Rom. 8:16–17). In the last verse of Romans 7, Paul gives thanks to Jesus Christ for His deliverance and commences

Romans 8 by writing, "There is no condemnation to those who are in Christ who do not walk according to the flesh but according to the Spirit."

If you have been born again of the Spirit of God, whatever your past life has been, your history is not your destiny. Your destiny is all in God's plan. Listen to His whispers and allow Him to fill your spirit with His revelation.

When writing to the Corinthian believers (1 Cor. 2), Paul writes that none of the rulers of the age when Christ was upon earth knew who He was; otherwise, they would not have crucified the Lord of Glory (1 Cor. 2:8). To this thought, he adds 1 Corinthians 2:9–12 in which verse nine is often misquoted; and by not continuing with verse ten, it is used out of context, verses 9-10…But as it is written: 'Eye has not seen nor ear heard. Nor have entered into the heart of man the things that God has prepared for those who love Him."

But God has revealed them to us through His Spirit. For the Spirit searches all things yes the deep things of God. The truth is that God is revealing truth to us by His Holy Spirit.

In order to explain this, Paul asks the question *For what man knows the things of a man except the Spirit of the man which is in him?* The spirit of man, as already stated, is the part of man that is resurrected at the new birth and is eternal. Our spirit is who we are. If it were possible for someone to examine our spirit or dissect it from the rest of our being, it would reveal exactly what we are really like.

To understand and really know God, we too would need His Spirit because it is His Spirit and His Spirit alone that has this revelation. The truth and the good news that Paul is teaching is found in 1 Corinthians 2:12: "Now we have received not the spirit of the world but the Spirit who is from God, that we might know the things that have been given to us by God."

It is the eyes of the unbeliever that has not seen, it is his ears that have not heard, and it his heart that these truths have not entered. But God is revealing them to us by His Spirit. Praise God for the revelation that comes by the Holy Spirit, who is not only the guarantee of our salvation but the one who is opening our understanding to the things that God, in His grace and love, has prepared for those who love Him.

This the Gospel that we preach!

6

The Gospel We Preach
Is the Gospel of the Grace of God

The grace of God is one of the major differences between Christianity and any other religion. The Gospel of the grace of God offers everyone salvation despite what sins they may have committed because the very nature of grace has nothing to do with works as far as receiving salvation is concerned. How anyone can be mistaken or be deceived as to this central theme of the Gospel is quite amazing. Yet we still have preached from many pulpits "the good works" gospel. The sad truth is that multitudes walk out of their churches week by week believing that on the basis of their own efforts and morality, they can earn salvation and one day make it to heaven.

The very word, *grace*, has several different meanings; and to limit it to the most popular usage of the word is to do it a disservice. The Greek word *Charis* means "something that affords joy, pleasure, delight, etc." It also means good will, loving kindness, and mercy— the kindness of a master to a slave. It is also used to depict God's kindness bestowed upon someone undeserving.

When asked to give a definition of *grace*, most people would probably answer, "God's unmerited favor." That, of course, would definitely be one usage of the word and would fit into the biblical verses where the NT makes clear that salvation is by grace alone.

The apostle Paul, when reminding the Ephesian believers of their journey in faith—from being spiritually dead in sin and being dominated by their own sinful lusts (Eph. 2)—brings them to that wonderful verse "But God" (Eph. 2:4). Every believer needs to continually remind themselves of where they have come from and where they might have been had it not been for a "but God" intervention in their life. Some were once sleeping rough on the streets, victims of drug abuse, and others might have been working the streets under the control of a pimp. The bars of a prison cell would have restricted others to doing time. Still, others would have simply lived for the "American dream," and all their energies would have been swallowed up by the desire for more wealth and possessions. Then there are the millions who were once deceived into believing salvation was by doing good works. There are many more scenarios that could be mentioned, but all real believers—no matter what their story—can say, "This is where I once was 'but God.'" Thank God for His interventions and His revelation of *grace*.

Keep in mind these passages:

> But God who is rich in mercy because of His great love with which He loved us, even when we were dead in trespasses, made us alive together with Christ [by grace you have been saved]. (Eph. 2:4–5)
>
> For by grace are you have been saved through faith, and that not of yourselves; it is the gift of God, not of works lest anyone should boast. (Eph. 2:8–9)

The only works that are mentioned here is "His workmanship" (Eph. 2:10) creating believers in Christ Jesus for good works.

These are two scriptures that back up this teaching:

- Being justified freely by His grace through the redemption that is in Christ Jesus. (Rom. 3:24)

- I marvel that you are turning away so soon from Him who called you into the grace of Christ to a different gospel, which is not another, but there are some who trouble you and want to pervert the gospel of Christ. (Gal. 1:6–7)

The Galatians were in danger of being led astray back into legalism, which was contrary to the gospel of grace. The very thing they had come out of—that of seeking to please God by fulfilling the law—they were now being drawn back into by false teachers. Paul makes clear that this is a different gospel and perverts the true one! Take note of these verses:

For the grace of God that brings salvation has appeared to all men. (Tit. 2:11)

As each one has received a gift, minister it to one another as good stewards of the manifold grace of God. (1 Pet. 4:10)

The "grace of God" has many facets to it, some of which we will look at later, but as far as salvation is concerned, it is by "grace and not by works." God's unmerited favor, unearned favor, is bestowed upon the repentant sinner and has nothing to do with self-effort, giving to charity, or by how many times we have attended church or any other so-called good works. It is by *grace*. There can be no boasting on our part, only thankfulness and praise that the God who saved us by His grace deserves all the praise we can give Him.

The apostle Paul was definitely a candidate for the grace of God because he was the biggest enemy of the church before his conversion. Paul was a religious Pharisee who believed he was doing God a favor by persecuting those who followed Jesus Christ. It was Paul who, in Acts 7:58, looked after the clothes of those who stoned Stephen outside Jerusalem.

Saul, as he was then called, heard Stephen's sermon; watched him die at the hands of an angry, demon-frenzied mob; and heard him say in his last moments on earth the incredible words recorded in Acts 7:56: "Look I see heaven opened and the Son of Man standing at the right hand of God." As the last stones hit his now-bruised and broken body, his last words were "Lord, do not charge them with this sin." Saul actually witnessed the first Christian martyr who, like Jesus, had asked for forgiveness for his murderers. Little did Paul realize at that moment that the eternal seed had been sown in to his life through Stephen. The Word of God has the power to transform and revolutionize anyone's heart. Saul was on God's hit list, and he didn't know it! The blood of the martyr was not spilled in vain and never is.

In Acts 8, Saul had consented to Stephen's death. Although he had not hurled a rock at the preacher, he was guilty as any who had. It was after this that great persecution broke out against the followers of Jesus. Believers were scattered throughout the regions of Judea and Samaria, except the apostles. It seemed the one who was at the head of the persecution was none other than Saul himself. He was brutal, showed no mercy, and he hated the Christ followers; he had both men and women dragged off to prison simply because they were Christians. He did not seem to be bothered by his conscience; he burned inside with anger and was blind to the message of the Gospel they preached.

There was great fear in the hearts of the Christ followers. Saul was a hunter on a mission to exterminate the church, no matter what it took and what the consequences were. He wreaked havoc of the church (Acts 8:3). The devil always overplays his hand! Although the church was scattered, so was the Gospel message they preached. The Gospel went with them! It was similar to scattering coals of fire. Unless the fire is extinguished first, it will spread. That is exactly what happened to the church. Believers with the fire of a holy passion for lost souls simply spread the fire. The region was under siege of the Gospel (Acts 8:4). Philip went down to Samaria and preached Christ to them; and multitudes believed, many were healed, and great joy was in the city. It was Jesus Himself who had preached to the Samaritans after His conversation with the woman at the well (John 4), many believed (John 4:39).

Once again, we see the power of the Word. Jesus had exhorted His disciples to "lift up their eyes and see that the fields were white unto harvest" (John 4:35). Maybe at that moment, He was looking beyond the crowd that had gathered to a time in the future when Philip would come with signs and wonders and the preaching of the Gospel.

Although Saul was still "breathing out threats and murder against the believers," it is in Acts 9 we have the record of his conversion. He meets the Christ who he had refused to believe in. I have heard it said that God is a "gentleman." By that, I presume it is meant that He would never force Himself on anyone against their will. However, what takes place in Acts 9 seems to contradict such a statement.

On his way to Damascus, Paul was intent on having more believers arrested and brought back to Jerusalem, but Jesus inter-vened. Saul met a "but God" moment! A bright light shone around him, causing him to fall to the ground. And then an audible voice—this was not one of God's whispers; this was a voice of authority that demanded his attention—came with a question, "Saul, why are you persecuting Me?" Saul met the question with a question. "Who are you, Lord?" "I am Jesus whom you are persecuting." This is interest-ing, to say the least, and demands we just stop and consider such a statement.

Saul had been persecuting the church, but Jesus told him that Saul had actually been persecuting Him! Here, we have the wonder-ful revelation that Christ and the church are one; they are eternally united. What God has joined together let no man put asunder. He is the head of the church, and the church is His body. You can't have one without the other. This is one of the greatest themes of the NT. We are "in Christ"—joint heirs with Him, buried with Him in bap-tism, and rose with Him in newness of life.

Jesus made it clear here to Saul that when you touch the church you touch Me. Persecute the church, you persecute Me. One can only imagine what must have been racing through Saul's mind at that moment! Before he could put his thoughts together to make any sense of that, another question came to him from the Lord of glory: "Is it hard for you to kick against the goads?" The goad was an instrument used by farmers to keep the oxen as they were plowing the fields in a straight line. If they started to wander, the farmer would use the goad (a stick, sometimes ten feet long with a sharp end to it). When the oxen felt the prick of the goad, then it would get the message it was wandering off course.

Saul had blindly gone his own way, but the Lord had been seeking to bring him in to line with the truth, but he had kicked against it. He had refused to pay attention to Stephen's message. He had refused to find the miracles that had been happening in Jerusalem authentic. As far as the resurrection was concerned, that was a made-up story that had no credibility. But then the resurrected Christ speaks to the greatest human enemy of the church, and Saul is reduced to trembling! "Lord, what do you want me to do?" was Saul's question.

From the moment of his new birth, Saul wanted to know what he was to do. Paul was led into Damascus as a blind man, but his spiritual eyes were opening wide. This was a man whose name would be known by demons, who would one day lay down his life to the executioner. Before that time, cities would be shaken with the Gospel, churches would be planted, souls saved, special miracles would pave the way to great revivals. This was Saul who became known as the apostle Paul and who called himself the "chief of sinners" who preached and taught the grace of God.

There was no one with better credentials to preach about the undeserved favor of God!

When Jesus told the story of the prodigal son, He was teaching many things, one of which was the Father's love even though the son didn't deserve it. The prodigal son was coming home knowing he had sinned against heaven and his father. What a picture it is painted in this story—the father rushing out to meet his son, the prodigal coming home in shame and guilt, the father rushing out to meet him with love that he didn't deserve!

A robe, ring, and a pair of shoes had been placed aside waiting for this day and the fatted calf too, although he would not be too happy! This was just a welcome home, and the father threw a party. What a picture of "grace"! This was forgiveness with blessings thrown in. That is exactly what the grace of God is really all about. It is not simply forgiveness for undeserving sinners but promotion to become sons and daughters of God. That is amazing. That is why it is "amazing grace"!

Grace has a much wider definition than just "undeserved favor." Grace is also something we are encouraged to grow in. "But grow in the grace and knowledge of our Lord and Savior Jesus Christ," as said in 2 Peter 3:18.

The apostle Paul prayed three times regarding his thorn in the flesh (2 Cor. 12:7–10). Because of his abundance of revelation, the Lord wanted to protect him from pride, and God allowed a messenger of Satan to buffet him. God said to him, "My grace is sufficient for you, for My strength is made perfect in weakness."

The grace of God is also a strengthening grace that can come to the believer when in the natural we may feel weak. The valleys and storms of life that we all pass through as we journey through a broken world are things that can emotionally drain us. Situations that we can't fix in the natural, outside of God's grace and strengthening, can affect us to such a degree that we may wonder if we will ever come through; but somehow, He draws us close and we experience the strengthening of His grace. Paul uses a term in 2 Corinthians 1:8–9, which says,

> We were burdened beyond measure, above strength so that we despaired even of life. Yes, we had the sentence of death in ourselves that we should not trust in ourselves but in God who raises the dead.

Paul does not mention the grace of God in these verses, but we can be sure that is exactly what he experienced!

The grace of God also gives us the ability to operate beyond our own strength. Paul encourages the church at Corinth to be liberal in their giving, to help the believers that were in need. He does this by referring to the churches of Macedonia (2 Cor. 8) on whom the Lord had bestowed His grace. Despite the great trials and afflictions and also deep poverty, they abounded in liberality. Notice 2 Corinthians 8:3–4: "For I bear witness that according to their ability, yes and beyond their ability they were freely willing, imploring us with much urgency that we would receive the gift and the fellowship of the ministering to the saints." Notice "Beyond their ability." The grace of God was so much that beyond their own ability, they gave, they believed, they ministered to others' needs. No wonder Peter urges the believers to "grow in grace."

Hebrews 4:16 tells us, "Let us come boldly to the throne of *grace* [my italics] that we may obtain mercy and find grace to help in time of need." What a comforting thought that the throne of God is called the "throne of grace." We are encouraged to come boldly—not timidly with our heads bowed in fear, but *boldly*—in confidence and faith. In our times of need, we are assured there is a God of Grace and a throne of grace and mercy waiting to strengthen and help us.

Paul begins his letter to the Corinthian church in 1 Corinthians 1:3 with "Grace to you and peace from God our Father and the Lord Jesus Christ."

First, with grace, that is how it all begins. Without it, we would be eternally lost; but with it, we have favor with the God of the universe whom we are bidden to call our Father.

This the Gospel we preach.

7

Declared Righteous

The apostle Paul takes us on a journey through the book of Romans. He states the fact that we have all sinned and fallen short of God's glory (Rom. 3:23) and expounds this truth in the first few chapters of his letter. Take note of this passage:

> For the wrath of God is revealed from heaven against all ungodliness and unrighteousness of men who suppress the truth in unrighteousness, because what may be known of God is manifest in them for God has shown it to them. (Rom. 1:18–19)

We must always remember that while grace awaits the repentant sinner, the holiness of God hates sin so much that He was willing to allow His Son to take the full judgment of our sins upon Himself when His Son died on the cross. If we embrace by faith this truth, we receive the grace of God. The sinner who refuses His grace will face His wrath.

Notice the phrase "who suppress the truth in unrighteousness" (v. 18). Truth is all around us and is within us. Take note of this passage:

> What may be known of God is manifest in them for God has shown it to them. For since the creation

of the world, His invisible attributes are clearly seen, being understood by the things that are made, even His eternal power and Godhead, so they are without excuse. (Rom. 1:19–20)

The following verses tell us that although they knew God, they refused to give Him the honor and glory that is His; and as a result, their foolish hearts were darkened. They then changed the image of God into idols. The degeneration that happened was as a result of the fact that "they suppressed the truth in unrighteousness." *To suppress* is basically "to hold down"; "to subdue"; "to crush." This is what they had done with the truth. Millions today still do the same, yet God has written His attributes into creation. They are everywhere for the eye to see, but instead of believing the truth, many still choose to suppress it. When you suppress the truth, idols take its place.

The first chapter of Romans is a sad commentary on a world that had been given so much by a loving Creator but would rather give itself to vile passions and idolatry. The Gospel is a message of God seeking sinners, chasing them with His love and grace; but everyone should be aware that there can be a time, as there was with the generation Paul spoke about in this first chapter of Romans, when God can draw the line! This is what we learn in these passages:

- God gave them up to uncleanness. (Rom. 1:24)
- God gave them up to vile passions. (Rom. 1:26)
- God gave them over to a debased mind. (Rom. 1:28)

I well remember our Bible college principal, Mr. John Carter, relating a story of when he was visiting Ireland many years ago. He witnessed a man sitting by a peat fire; and as they were talking, the man reached into the fire and picked out one of the peat coals and placed it on to the hearth. The coal was hot, of course, but his fingers were not burned. His explanation was that he had done that so many times that his fingers had become calloused and hardened, so much so that he didn't really notice how hot the coal was!

It is possible for someone to suppress the truth and refuse the overwhelming witness of God so many times that they become hardened in their hearts and minds. They no longer hear or feel the tug of God's love urging them to the cross and to salvation. One day, of course, there will be a final line drawn, whether at death or when the great judgment takes place. The day of grace will be over, and multitudes will recognize there is no way back anymore! Seize the day while you have the opportunity.

The question *What happens to those who have never heard the Gospel?* is often asked. I have also heard it said that when people have heard the Gospel and refuse to respond to the Lord, they are without excuse. If that is true, then it is almost better for some if they never hear! The real truth is that there is no one without excuse, whether they have heard the Gospel or not, because God has written Himself into creation (Rom. 1:20).

We can be sure that on judgment day, the judge of all the earth will judge righteously.

The good news of the Gospel is that we can be declared righteous although we have all sinned.

When referring to the law that was given to Moses on Sinai, Paul says,

> Whatever the law says, it says to those who are under the law, that every mouth may be stopped and all the world may become guilty before God. Therefore by the deeds of the law no flesh will be justified in His sight, for by the law is the knowledge of sin … But the righteousness of God apart from the law is revealed being witnessed by the law and the prophets, even the righteousness of God through faith in Jesus Christ to all and on all who believe, for there is no difference; for all have sinned and fall short of the glory of God. (Rom. 3:19–20, 21–23)

There is a "righteousness" that can be imputed which is not given on the basis of our efforts at keeping the Ten Commandments. This is not an earned righteousness because Paul has already made clear we can't earn it—we have all sinned!

So what kind of righteousness does the Gospel of Jesus Christ offer?

It is the *righteousness of God* through faith in Jesus Christ to all and on all who believe. There is no difference whether Jew or Gentile, whatever nationality, background, or past history.

So let us look a little closer to what is offered through faith in Jesus Christ.

God never changes as perfection doesn't need to change. He is righteous, always will be, and always has been. There are no flaws in His character, dark spots, or imperfections. The Psalms declare His glory and honor. The angels cry "Holy, holy, holy." The devil could not point the finger at Christ, and Jesus could say, "The prince of this world comes, but he finds nothing in Me." He was perfect and flawless.

Jesus said, "He that has seen Me has seen the Father."

It is the very righteousness of God that is on offer. The deepest dyed sinner can be declared *righteous*, not simply forgiven but flawless!

To illustrate this amazing truth, Paul uses the story of Abraham. The Jews revered Abraham as their father; it was through Abraham that the nation of Israel was born. God was known as the God of Abraham, Isaac, and Jacob.

"Abraham believed God and it was counted to him for righteousness," the Bible says in Romans 4:3. Abraham had nothing to boast about because this righteousness was not given on the basis of His works but on the basis of faith.

It is impossible by trying to keep the law (the Ten Commandments) that anyone can be justified ("just as if they had never sinned") because it is the law that brings us the knowledge of sin. We look at the commandments and have to readily admit we have broken so many! (Rom. 3:20).

The Gospel message is that there is a righteousness that is apart from the law that is imputed to the repentant sinner through faith in Jesus Christ. (Rom. 3:22).

We have the word *propitiation* (v. 25) by His blood. When Jesus poured out His blood on the cross, He *satisfied* the holiness of God; and the God who is just was then justified in offering justification to the sinner.

God Himself demonstrated His righteousness—His character never changes—but in order to offer us salvation and to declare us righteous and justified in His sight, Christ had to take our judgment. He had to satisfy the holiness of God!

This excludes any boasting, any pride in our own works or accomplishments, because this righteousness is not given to us on the basis of our own merit. Our only boast is in the cross.

In order to back up his argument and teaching, Paul turns to the OT story of Abraham. Paul calls him "our father." The Jews revered him, the nation had descended from him, what better illustration could Paul use, and Abraham was the perfect example.

Abraham believed God, and it was accounted to him for righteousness (Rom. 4:3). The word *accounted* or *imputed* does not mean that Abraham became righteous automatically. This does not mean that Abraham was righteous in character and conduct from the moment he believed, he still had his flaws and made his mistakes but it means that God looked upon him as righteous because of his faith. As with so many of the characters mentioned in the Bible, we see their flaws as well as their good points. The Bible hides nothing. It is said of Napoleon when he was having his portrait painted that he said, "Paint me warts and all."

Abraham, looking for the fulfillment of the promise of a son, chose one day to sleep with his maid, thinking this was possibly the way God would fulfill His promise to the aged couple. That decision was one that eventually led to great friction between Sarah and Hagar the maid and resulted in Hagar and her son having to leave and become outcasts. Abraham, like the rest of us, had nothing to boast in and knew very well that becoming righteous in God's sight was through faith and by God's grace.

To refuse this offer and to try and earn salvation by works is to be declared to be in debt. The debt can never be erased by self-effort, only by faith in Christ.

When the prodigal son returned home, he was given a new robe, and this robe covered his rags and dirt and was just one token of his father's love. When Abraham believed and placed his faith in the living God, he was given an invisible robe of righteousness. He didn't appear any different to others; but to God, he was now viewed as righteous, flawless. All of this took place one evening recorded for us in Genesis 15. Abraham complains that he has no offspring, no heir, but God assured him that his heir would be one that would come from his own body (Gen. 15:4). He took Abraham outside and showed him the stars and promised him he would be blessed with many descendants. It was as Abraham gazed into the heavens, the same heavens that His Father God had created that he believed God, and it was accounted to him for righteousness (Gen. 15:6).

Faith declared him flawless, justified, and righteous; but God is never satisfied, declaring us righteous. His purpose is then to work on our character so that righteousness is outworked in our lives.

To inherit the land, Abraham had to obey—he had to follow, he had to walk before the Lord with faith and obedience. Without obedience, he would not have inherited the promised land. Faith in Christ renders us flawless, and obedience brings us to life change and righteousness being outworked.

The epistle of James is very practical and, of course, is well known for its theme of faith and works. "Faith without works is dead," as said in James 2:17. The epistle commences with the exhortation to have joy amid trials and testing, knowing that the testing of faith produces patience (v. 3). James desires that the believers for which he is writing become mature and lack nothing when it comes to Christian character. He exhorts the believers to pray for wisdom so that in and through all the hardships and trials, they would understand that God is still at work and is still sovereign.

As you read through this epistle, there are many exhortations to put aside all unrighteousness and wickedness. Partiality must not be shown to the rich and well-dressed while the poor are neglected. He also deals with the tongue and gossip and what a fire that can start. With these things in mind, it is pretty obvious that obedience is needed and not just faith! Does everything just fall into place and the believer automatically live a righteous life? Obviously not. Otherwise, James would not go to the great lengths he does in this epistle calling believers to live righteously.

It is in this same epistle that at first glance there seems to be an apparent contradiction between what Paul teaches in Romans (justification by faith alone) and what James teaches—that is, a man is justified by works and not by faith only (James 2:24).

James is concerned with believers not allowing sin to mar their progress into maturity and for their faith to be manifested by righteous works and acts. The testimony of Christ can so easily be spoiled by people professing to know Christ but living as though they have never met Him!

We have all heard the excuse as to why some never attend church because there are too many hypocrites. The sad fact is, there are! The believer can either become a living Bible or a living libel! Of course, you can't have the false without the genuine. The problem is that all too often the unbeliever sees only the false. James is exhorting the believers to show genuine faith by their lifestyle and works.

Paul teaches that we are justified by faith before God. James teaches that we are justified by works before men. No contradiction but rather a complementation.

The Christian singing group Mercy Me wrote a song called "Flawless." The chorus line goes this way:

> No matter the hurts, no matter the bruises,
> No matter the pain, still the truth is,

The cross has made,
The cross has made me flawless.

What an amazing truth to be declared flawless, righteous, in the sight of a holy God. When the believer approaches the throne of grace, he or she is not entering the throne room of God's presence with the filth of past sins on show but with the robe of Christ's righteousness.

We enter flawless, and there we make our requests known.

This is the Gospel we preach.

8

Redemption

I used to wonder why Paul and his missionary party were forbidden by the Holy Spirit to go to Bithynia (Acts 16). After all, hadn't Jesus given the command to go into all the world? It seems the master strategist, the Holy Spirit, had other plans. When turning to the first epistle of Peter, we find the opening verses reveal the answer. He writes to the believers in Bithynia, so obviously, the Holy Spirit had someone else for that task and redirected Paul.

It is in the first chapter of Peter's epistle that we find the word *redeemed*:

> Knowing that you were not redeemed with corruptible things like silver and gold, from your aimless conduct received by tradition from your fathers, but with the precious blood of Christ, as of a lamb without blemish and without spot. (1 Pet. 1:18–19)

The revelation of the blood runs through both Old and New Testaments—in fact, we have to look no further than Genesis and the Garden of Eden to see the first reference to this. Before considering this, let us consider what the word *redeemed* actually means.

The Greek word *lutroo* is derived from *lutron* or *lytron*, which is derived from *luo*—which means "to loosen that which is bound"—

similar to the picture of a slave market where the slave is bound awaiting someone to pay the required amount for his services. The noun *lutron* is the ransom price paid for loosing captives from their bonds and setting them free. The verb *lutroo* refers to the setting free of a captive or slave on the receipt of a ransom payment.

In the Roman Empire, there were many slaves and slave markets; but to set a slave free, there was always a ransom payment that had to be made.

It is said of Abraham Lincoln that he ventured into a slave market one day and purchased a slave girl. He took her outside and told her he was letting her go free, much to the astonishment of the girl. She was so overawed by this act of kindness, she offered to go back to his home and serve him willingly. This, of course, was not what Lincoln had in mind; he simply wanted to demonstrate his belief that all people, no matter what the color of their skin, should be free.

When we understand that an eternal ransom price has been paid by the blood of Jesus Christ, we too should want to serve Him for the rest of our lives.

Peter teaches us that a price has been paid for our eternal souls, and it wasn't silver or gold. No amount of money could pay this ransom price—blood was demanded. Calvary was the place, Jesus was the sacrifice, and it was His blood that was poured out in order that we could be loosed, taken out of the slave market of sin, and set free. Peter calls Jesus's blood "precious blood" as of a lamb without blemish and without spot.

To return to the first time we see blood used in a sacrifice, we must return to the book of Genesis. The awful consequences of Adam's sin and rebellion became apparent with the whole of creation in total unrest and fear. Thorns and thistles sprang up from the earth, and the thorns and thistles of sin had also taken root in the human heart and mind. Can anyone imagine the anguish of Adam as he had to explain to his children that there was a time when everything lived in harmony and God's voice would commune with him in the cool of the evening?

Although the Bible does not tell us that God had made clear to Adam that any approach toward Him by a sacrifice must be one of blood, He does make it abundantly clear when He only accepts Abel's sacrifice. Also, God must have shed blood and killed two animals to provide a covering for Adam and Eve's nakedness after they had sinned.

The two brothers, Cain and Abel, both brought an offering to the Lord (Gen. 4). Cain brought of the fruit of the ground (Gen. 4:3). Abel was a keeper of the sheep, and he brought the firstborn of the flock and of their fat (Gen. 4:2). The Lord respected Abel and his offering but did not respect Cain or his offering (v. 4). The result was Cain was very angry and, in his anger, killed his brother Abel.

Adam saw firsthand in his own family the effect of fallen nature. Abel's offering was a blood sacrifice, and it was accepted; Cain's offering was the produce of his own labors. The book of Hebrews tells us that Abel's sacrifice was a more excellent sacrifice than Cain's through which he obtained witness that he was righteous, God testifying of his gifts (Heb. 11:4).

Today, millions of people in religions across the world are still striving for acceptance by their particular gods by self-effort. Our own works will never be sufficient, and anything we may do, no matter how commendable in the eyes of the world, all fall short of gaining God's respect. Anything apart from the blood of Christ disannuls the cross, the greatest plan and sacrifice the universe has ever seen.

Life is in the blood.

When Noah received the word of the Lord immediately after the flood, God told him that every moving thing that lives would be food for him but he was not to eat the flesh with its life—that is, its blood (Gen 9:3–4). We also find in the Law of Moses, recorded in Leviticus 17, several verses referring to the life of the flesh is in the blood (Gen. 9:11–14).

Anyone who has ever lost any amount of blood will readily vouch for this truth. To lose blood is to become anemic, to lose strength, to become dizzy, and to feel that your life is draining away.

That is exactly what is happening because our life is in our blood. When we consider this, we have to recognize that when Jesus poured out His blood—and I use the word *poured* rather than *spilled* because to spill something is an accident—to pour something out is a deliberate act. Jesus Christ, in His great love for us, freely and willingly poured out His blood, His life, for our sins. When Paul declares that Christ gave Himself for us, he is actually teaching that Christ gave His life for us. Our life is in the blood.

The OT is littered with blood sacrifices. As previously stated, all these sacrifices pointed to the one great sacrifice that was to come; they were simply shadows and types. Without going into any in depth study of the offerings that are taught in the book of Leviticus, we need to understand that there were various types of offerings—e.g., burnt offering, meat offering, peace offering, the sin offering, the trespass offering.

It is interesting to note that as Abraham was about to offer Isaac upon the altar of sacrifice as God tested him (Gen. 22), His hand was stayed from slaying his son by the word from heaven, "Do not lay your hand on the lad." Previous to this, Isaac had asked, "Where is the lamb for a burnt offering?" Abraham answered, "My son God will provide Himself a lamb for a burnt offering."

The basic difference between the *burnt offering* and the *sin offering* was that the burnt offering was the offering that was brought by the offerer for acceptance as a worshipper; it was to be a sweet savor unto the Lord which would satisfy Him. The sin offering was brought by the sinner to pay the penalty of sin and trespass.

The lamb that Abraham spoke of that God would provide as a burnt offering was, of course, Jesus who satisfied the Father in everything He did and became the "propitiation" for us (Rom. 3:25), the One who appeased the Father's judgment by His blood. His whole life was a sweet-smelling savor to the Father. Through His sinless, pure, and perfect life, He became the perfect, sinless sacrifice who satisfied God's holiness and on the cross bore the full judgment of a holy and righteous God. Jesus fulfilled both these types, the burnt offering and the sin offering. If His life had not been a sweet-smelling savor before His Father continually, He could not have become our sin offering.

Paul exhorts the Ephesian believers in Ephesians 5:2: "Walk in love, as Christ also has loved us and gave Himself for us, as an offering and a sacrifice to God for a sweet smelling aroma."

We are to walk in the kind of love that is willing to weep with those who weep and rejoice with those who rejoice. Love that moves us with compassion like the Good Samaritan who was willing to bind up the wounds and pay for the lodging of the man who had been beaten up and robbed. Love that regards others more highly than ourselves. The love that Paul describes in 1 Corinthians 13 is the kind of love by which the world will know that we are true believers—unselfish love that centers on Christ, His will and purpose for our lives, which makes His agenda our agenda.

Jesus asked Peter three times, "Peter, do you love me more than these?" (John 21:15). After a frustrating night of fishing and catching nothing, Jesus was waiting on the shore. He knew all the frustrations in Peter's heart and mind. This happened during the period between Christ's resurrection and ascension. Peter was probably wondering what the future held for him and how they would survive. Everything was not crystal-clear in his mind, and Jesus had appeared and disappeared on a number of occasions and maybe he wondered if His last appearance was actually His last. Whatever was going through Peter's mind, one thing is certain: he said, "I am going fishing." We all need to realize that we influence others in whatever we do whether it is for good or bad. When Peter made his way to the boat, other disciples followed!

I thank God for those who, down the years, have made an impact upon my life and have affected me for good. People who in church congregations, despite all their difficulties and trials, have remained faithful to the Lord and His church. I vividly remember a funeral service of a young mother in her early thirties. As the casket was being taken down the aisle, her Father walked behind with his arms raised to heaven, praising God and thanking Him for a wonderful daughter.

Others have challenged me to believe God and exercise faith. In the times when my wife and I have gone through our deepest valleys and trials, we have thanked God for the phone calls of encouragement the notes, emails, and letters. Some people are just good to be around; they are sweet-smelling savors of God's goodness and joy and are true inspirations. Yes, we all influence others.

Despite Peter's negative effect and all his frustrations when he reached shore that morning, the Savior simply said, "Come and have breakfast." This was Jesus inviting the impetuous Peter who, several weeks before, had denied he knew Christ and now, in his frustration, had gone fishing. But the question must be settled whether or not Peter was to fulfill the destiny of God in his life. It was the most important question that could be asked—"Do you love Me?"

We must always keep at the forefront of our walk with the Lord, the knowledge that we are invited into a love relationship. God is a person, not some remote being. He is our Father, and to love Him is our greatest purpose. May it be our greatest desire. If you were to look into the eyes of the Savior over the flickering flames of a little fire as Peter did and you were asked the same question, what would your answer be? God still longs for the sweet-smelling savor of worship and service that springs from a passionate love relationship with Him.

Abraham said, "God will provide Himself a lamb for a burnt offering." The lamb was one of the animals used as a sin offering. In the sweet-savor offerings, the worshiper was coming before God for acceptance. In the sin offering, the sinner comes convicted and confessing his sin. During the journey of Israel through the wilderness on their way to the Promised Land, the tabernacle, or tent of meeting, was the center of their worship. The outer court of the tabernacle was the place where offerings and sacrifices were brought. The altar was the place where the animal would be killed.

Imagine for a moment an Israelite coming toward the tent of meeting. He has within his arms a lamb. He is coming for forgive-

ornness; he is bringing his sin offering.

ness; he is bringing his sin offering. He enters the gate of the outer court, and there, in full view, is the altar. The animal senses the fear and smells the blood that has been shed of other sacrifices.

I remember so well when I would take our black Labrador to the vet for his annual checkup and injections. He was so happy to be coming with me for a ride in the car, but the moment we got near the veterinary clinic, he sensed something and smelled something that made him start to tremble. At that point, all my dog training was to no avail. I had to literally drag him inside, and the only time he stopped trembling was when we were outside and on our way home!

The lamb that had been chosen was without blemish, healthy, and spotless. But this little lamb would be fighting for its life. No matter how it struggled, it was going to die, it would be tied to the horns of the altar, and then its throat would be cut. With its blood poured out, the sinner would lay his hands on the animal's head and confess his sins. It was as though his sin then passed to the offering (the lamb) and he was granted forgiveness. The innocent little lamb had become his substitute. Blood would be shed and death occurred.

Take note of this passage: "The life of the flesh is in the blood, and I have given it to you upon the altar to make atonement for your souls, for it is the blood that makes atonement for the soul" (Lev. 17:11). The book of Hebrews has so many OT symbols and types within its pages and is a great commentary. It parallels the OT and the NT. Someone well said, "The New is in the Old contained. The Old is by the New explained."

"According to the law almost all things are purified with blood, and without the shedding of blood there is no remission," as we learn in Hebrews 9:22.

Let's return to the time prior to the wilderness journeys of Israel when the Israelites were slaves in Egypt. God had chosen a man called Moses to be their deliverer. Moses had spent forty long years looking after sheep in the backside of the desert, which was not the most exciting place to spend one's days, before something unusual occurred. A bush began to burn but was not consumed. God has many ways of getting our attention, and monotonous days can suddenly change when God speaks and surprises us.

Moses had to understand that even in the desert, if God is present, it becomes holy ground. With his sandals taken off, he listens to the plan and destiny God had for his life. He couldn't have dared dream of what he was about to hear. God had chosen him to go back to Egypt to stand before the most powerful man on the face of the earth at that time, the mighty pharaoh. He was to demand, in the name of the Lord, that Israel should be freed.

Looking after sheep in the desert was child's play concerned with this. Talk about taking someone out of their comfort zone. This was definitely the extreme! Of course, like many of us, at the very thought of doing something way beyond our perceived abilities, we can make excuses or even argue with God. It didn't get Moses anywhere, although he tried! God had an answer to every excuse. To try and argue with God, we are on a loser because He is the Lord and He doesn't change!

Let's fast forward to the time when Moses stood before the mighty pharaoh and displayed miracle after miracle by the finger of God. Despite all of this, pharaoh's heart was hardened, and he did not want to let the Israelites go free.

Enough was enough. The time had come when judgment was coming upon the land, and Moses had to give clear instructions to the Israelites of what they were to do to avoid such judgment. All the Egyptian firstborn in the land, both man and beast, would be struck by the judgment of the Lord and would be killed, and all the gods of Egypt would come under divine judgment too as is written in Exodus 12:1–7:

> Now the Lord spoke to Moses and Aaron in the land of Egypt, saying, "This month shall be your beginning of months, it shall be the first month of the year to you. Speak to all the congregation of Israel, saying; "On the tenth day of this month every man shall take

for himself a lamb, according to the house of his father, a lamb for a household. If the household is too small for the lamb, let him and his neighbor next to his house take it according to the number of persons; according to each man's need you shall make your count for the lamb. Your lamb shall be without blemish, a male of the first year. You may take it from the sheep or from the goats. Now you shall keep it until the fourteenth day of the same month. Then the whole assembly of the congregation of Israel shall kill it at twilight. And they shall take some of the blood and put it upon the two doorposts and on the lintel of the houses where they eat it.

I want you to notice how the lamb is referred to in verses 3–5:

- "Every man shall take for himself a lamb" (v. 3).
- "And if the household is too small for the lamb" (v. 4).
- "Your lamb shall be without blemish" (v. 5).

Many people regard Jesus as someone, like many others at that time, who was crucified for the perceived crime they had committed (*a* lamb). Others believe He died for the sins of the world and was God's Son (*the* Lamb). Yet even this does not bring salvation. We have to go further. Jesus must become a personal Savior. He must become *your* Lamb.

If I had been asked the question *Did I believe Jesus died for the sins of the whole world?* prior to my conversion, my answer would have been *yes*; but that didn't change me. It didn't bring me into a relationship with God and the experience of being "born again." The day that happened was the day when I recognized Jesus had died for the sins of the world and for my sins. That day, He became *my* Lamb. This is the question everyone must answer: Is Jesus Christ *a* lamb, *the* lamb, or is He *your* Lamb?

Imagine the father of the house smearing the lamb's blood on the doorposts and lintels. As he did, the blood would run down to the doorstep, which was like a basin. As he stood back, he would see the only way back into the house or out of the house was to pass through the blood.

The blood was to be the sign on their houses, and God had declared that when He would see the blood, He would pass over that household and the plague would not destroy them (Exod. 12:13).

God wasn't looking at the color of people's skin or what nationality they were; He was looking for one thing and one thing only—the blood of the lamb. The lamb was to be killed at twilight. The whole assembly shall kill it at twilight (Exod. 12:6). Notice again the word used is *it*. In God's eyes and God's master plan, there was only *one Lamb*—Jesus Christ!

This Passover was never to be forgotten, the people of Israel were commanded to keep this year by year, and in future generations, the children were to be reminded of this great event of deliverance (Exod. 12:24–27).

Throughout the OT, both in the tabernacle and later in the temple, sacrifices and offerings were made. When we turn to the NT, we have the announcement of John the Baptist. As Jesus was coming toward him, he said, "Behold the Lamb of God who takes away the sin of the world" (John 1:29).

Angels announced His birth, and John the Baptist announced His purpose. Here was the fulfillment of all the OT sacrifices; He had come from the throne of heaven clothed in human flesh. This was the Son of God and the son of man.

From this announcement, there would be just over three short years and the prophecy would be fulfilled, the Lamb of God would be slain!

Packed into those years would be many miracles, signs, and wonders, along with teachings and truths that would leave some of his hearers openmouthed. Others challenged in ways they had never been challenged before. He was bringing in a new Kingdom with totally different principles; He had demonstrated faith and authority and taught His disciples that they could do the same things if they would believe. He had upset the religious hierarchy, He had had spoken out against hypocrisy, and He had overthrown the money changers' tables in the courtyard of the Temple. He had reinforced the whole purpose of the temple that it was to be the house of prayer. He had wept at the tomb of his friend Lazarus and wept over Jerusalem because His own people had missed the days of visitation. For three and a half years, He had walked in the shadow of the cross, knowing one day He would fulfill His title as the Lamb of God.

John records in his Gospel account (John 19:14–16) that it was the preparation day of the Passover and about the sixth hour when they took Him away and crucified Him.

All four of the Gospels show us that Jesus was crucified on the preparation day of the Passover when the sacrificial lambs would be killed. Mark records that it was the third hour of the day. The Jewish day was reckoned from 6:00 a.m., so the third hour of the day would be 9:00 a.m. It was also at 9:00 a.m. that a special sacrifice was offered in the temple compound. The Jews were careful to ensure that not one of the bones of the sacrificial lamb or Passover lamb was broken. Only God could create a master plan like this, and only the Son of God could fulfill it!

Although it was customary to break the legs of those who had been crucified, this did not take place with Jesus neither was any of his bones broken, as we read in John 19:31-34 and Psalm 34:20. Historians tell us that certain prayers were offered in the temple during this particular time, one being a prayer for redemption. This prayer was actually being answered as Christ suffered and died as a lamb without spot and without blemish.

Paul, writing to the Corinthian church in 1 Corinthians 5:7, said, "For indeed Christ our Passover was sacrificed for us." What a truth this is, and Paul sums it all up by saying "Christ is our Passover." It is His blood that paid the price of redemption.

In Romans 3:23–24, Paul teaches that we have all sinned and fallen short of the glory of God, and in verse 24, we read, "Being justified freely by His grace through the redemption that is in Christ Jesus."

Please note that *grace* (undeserved favor) can only be offered on the basis of redemption, which is the price of Jesus's blood being poured out. If Christ had not paid that price, we would have no hope and would be eternally lost.

When Paul writes to the Colossian church in Colossians 1:13–14, he makes clear the truth that to be delivered and transferred from the domain of darkness into the Kingdom of God's dear Son is on the basis of redemption, which brings the forgiveness of sins.

In his teaching concerning the great hope and assurance that believers have regarding the coming of the Lord, Paul also mentions that the whole of creation is eagerly awaiting that day (Rom. 8:20–23). Through Adam's sin and rebellion, everything in creation was affected. The animal world was subject to fear and bondage.

Paul describes creation as being in labor pains, and believers too are inwardly groaning and awaiting Christ's appearing and the "redemption of the body." The redemption price that was paid through the blood of Christ was for spirit, soul, and body. A new body awaits every believer when Christ appears. We will explore this later when we deal with the subject of resurrection. To inwardly groan and long for something, that thing must be better than what we have already. Paul calls it "the glorious liberty of the children of God" (Rom. 8:21).

Jesus has become to us "wisdom from God and righteousness and sanctification and redemption that as it is written, 'He who glories let him glory in the Lord'" (1 Cor. 1:30–31).

The writer of the book of Hebrews also ensures us that this 'redemption' is eternal, and that He did not come with the blood of calves and goats.

Hebrews 9:12 says, "but with His own blood he entered the Most Holy Place *once and for all, having obtained eternal redemption* [my italics]."

The Gospel offers something far more than benefits in this life. It offers eternal redemption. When Jesus died and poured out His blood, our eternity was being paid for. Don't miss this greatest of offers. Your eternity is at stake.

This is the Gospel we preach.

9

Resurrection

The great "resurrection chapter" is found in Paul's first letter to the Corinthian Church, 1 Corinthians 15.

In the first four verses, we have a description of the Gospel that he preached:

> Moreover brothers I declare to you the Gospel which I preached to you, which also you received and in which you stand, by which also you are saved, if you hold fast the word which I preached to you unless you believed in vain. For I delivered to you first of all that which I also received that Christ died for our sins according to the scriptures, and that He was buried and that he rose again the third day according to the scriptures. (1 Cor. 15:1–4)

The resurrection of Jesus Christ is foundational to faith; after all, if He did not rise from the dead, then what do we have to rest our faith upon? As with all foundational doctrines, this one has come under great attack from the powers of hell. Foundations are extremely important. Without a good foundation, the whole structure is doomed to collapse. When building a house, the walls and structure are not allowed to be built until the building inspector has inspected the foundations.

Jesus told a story of two men who both built houses, the only difference being that one built his house upon sand the other upon rock. It was when the winds blew and the storm came that the house built upon sand collapsed. Jesus applied the story by showing us that His sayings or teachings have to be applied to our lives; otherwise, there is no firm foundation for our faith.

The teachings of Darwin attacked the creation story and taught that the human race evolved from mere animals (monkeys and apes). I must admit, I do like bananas, but nobody is going to make a monkey out of me! The problem was that this was believed and is still taught in our schools; the result is that once people believe they came from animals, they start behaving like them.

The breakdown of the family unit and the erosion of what was once clearly defined boundaries of marriage is another example of foundations being destroyed. Whenever there is a collapse of structure due to the erosion of foundations, there is always a mess. The church is called to move toward the mess with the answer, not run away from it.

The great apostle Paul, who had firsthand experience of hearing the voice of the risen Christ, was always ready to proclaim and defend the truth of the resurrection of Jesus Christ.

The newly formed churches in the NT had to be guarded from false teaching. Paul warned the elders of the Ephesian Church by saying,

> Take heed to yourselves and to all the flock, among which the Holy Spirit has made you overseers, to shepherd the church of God which He purchased with His own blood. For I know this that after my departure savage wolves will come in among you, not sparing the flock. (Acts 20:28–29)

The "savage wolves," as Paul calls them, were false teachers with false doctrine seeking to draw people to themselves. The Galatian

Church was also under attack from the teachings of those who were seeking to lure the believers back into a legalistic religion from which they had come out of and were freed. Paul's central message was "Stand fast in the liberty with which Christ has made you free and do not become entangled again with a yoke of bondage" (Gal. 5:1). Truth sets us free; it does not lead us into any kind of bondage.

Paul's appeal to the Corinthians was "How is it that some among you are saying there is no resurrection of the dead?" (1 Cor. 15:12). The Jews believed in the resurrection of the dead. Even Job, amid his trials, believed there would be a resurrection one day. Keep note of this passage: "For I know that my redeemer lives, and He shall stand at last on the earth: and after my skin is destroyed, this I know, that in my flesh I shall see God" (Job 19:25–26).

Jesus was asked questions concerning the resurrection by a group called the Sadducees. They did not believe in the resurrection and asked Him a question with the intention of trying to catch Him out in His words. The custom of that time was that if a man died who was married and he had no children, then his brother would marry the widow.

The question was that if this happened seven times within the one family, each brother died and the next brother in line took the widow again as his wife. When she eventually died, whose wife would she be in the resurrection? Jesus's answer was straight to the point: "In the resurrection they neither marry nor are given in marriage, but are like the angels of God in heaven" (Matt. 22:30). He didn't say they would not be male or female but simply they would not marry.

He then went to quote from Exodus 3:6 what God had said to Moses: "I am the God of Abraham the God of Isaac, and the God of Jacob." He then declared, "God is not the God of the dead, but of the living" (Matt. 22:23–32). This may sound at first contradictory; but when a believer dies, he or she is actually alive, ushered into the presence of God, who is the God of the living.

The miracle that really led to the events of crucifixion was the raising of Lazarus from the dead. Jesus, after hearing the news that His friend Lazarus was sick, eventually arrived at Bethany after Lazarus had died. Just before He raised him from the dead, He declared, "I am the resurrection and the life, he who believes in Me, though he may die, he shall live and whoever lives and believes in Me shall never die" (John 11:25–26).

This miracle stirred up the hatred of the religious hierarchy, and it was not too long before Jesus, who had raised Lazarus from the dead, was laid in a cold tomb having been crucified. But the Gospel we preach doesn't end there—it can't—otherwise, there would be no hope, no good news. The One who had declared Himself to be the resurrection and the life proved His words to be truth by rising from the dead three days later.

This changed everything, this news revolutionized the disciples and moved them from fear to faith, and this was the news that all hell wanted to suppress and keep under wraps. But that was impossible, a miracle had happened, and this same Jesus was to make many resurrection appearances during the length of the next forty days before he ascended to heaven. This truth then became foundational to apostolic preaching.

As Peter stood to address the crowds that had gathered on the day of Pentecost in Jerusalem, he delivers a message that would convict his hearers of their sin but would also point them to the cross where sins were paid for by the sacrifice of Christ. He then boldly declared that God had raised this same Jesus they had crucified from the dead because it was not possible that he should be held by death (Acts 2:22–24).

Peter then went on to quote from what David had written in the Old Testament concerning Christ:

> I foresaw the Lord always before my face, for He is at my right hand that I may not be shaken. Therefore my heart rejoiced and my tongue was glad; moreover my flesh also will rest in hope. For you will not leave my soul in Hades, nor will you allow your Holy One to see corrup-

tion. You have made known to me the ways of life; You will make me full of joy in Your presence. (Acts 2:25–28)

Peter expounds this scripture to his hearers by saying the verse could not refer to David for he is dead and that his tomb was still with them but, rather, that David was a prophet and he foresaw this and prophesied of the resurrection of Christ.

It is interesting to note that as David prophesied concerning Christ, he was saying that Christ continually lived with the Lord always before His face (Acts 2:25). In other words, for anyone to live in that manner, they have nothing to hide. Jesus lived a pure, sinless life and maintained the most intimate relationship with His Father. Death had no legal hold upon Him; He was sinless. It could not claim His life and therefore could not keep Him in the grave. Jesus had said that no one could take His life from Him, and no one did. He freely laid it down in order to take it up again.

If you think about it, how could the resurrection and the life remain in the grave? Peter declared "It was impossible that He should be held by death" (Acts 2:24).

This was the message the apostles preached and the message the world needs to hear again. The Christ who walked the shores of Galilee is still the same Jesus. The Jesus who healed the sick, cast out demons, and raised the dead is still the same Jesus and is very much alive.

After the healing of the lame man (Acts 3), Peter and John seized the opportunity to preach the Gospel again with similar words to that preached in Acts 2. They were quick to point out that the healing of the lame man was through faith in Christ's name and He is the one who God raised from the dead, and they were now His witnesses (Acts 3:15–16).

When Peter and John were brought before the authorities concerning the miracle of healing of the lame man, again, they witnessed to the resurrection of Christ (Acts 4:10–12). They were told they were not to teach or preach in the name of Jesus. As Peter and John were allowed to go free, they returned to the community of believers, and a remarkable prayer meeting took place.

With one accord, all the believers lifted their voices to God and prayed for signs and wonders and for boldness to declare the message. The very place where they were praying shook with the power and presence of God, and the result was that with great power, the apostles gave witness to the resurrection of the Lord Jesus. And great grace was upon them all (Acts 4:33).

Once again, the apostles were in trouble with the high priest (Acts 5:28–32). He told them they had filled Jerusalem with their doctrine. What a compliment! If only our Jerusalems were all filled with the same doctrine, what results we would see!

Unless the seed of the Word is sown, it cannot multiply. With the threats that they should not teach or preach in the name of Jesus, there answer was "We must obey God rather than men" (Acts 5:29). Although scripture teaches us to obey those authorities that God has set over us when earthly authority demands this, we have to obey a higher authority. The apostles were committed to the spread of this Gospel that proclaims a risen Savior.

Stephen became the first Christian martyr when he was stoned to death outside Jerusalem, and as he was dying, he said, "Look I see the heavens opened and the son of man standing at the right hand of God" (Acts 7:56). They cried out with a loud voice, stopped their ears, and ran at him with one accord, casting their clothes at the feet of a young man called Saul. It was when they heard of the resurrection that outraged them. The resurrection proved they were guilty of murdering the Christ of God. While all this was taking place, there was a young man called Saul who looked after their clothes while the raging mob threw rocks at Stephen until he breathed his last breath on earth. Saul heard it all, the eternal seed was sown into his heart, and, eventually, with a personal meeting of the resurrected Christ, he would become the great apostle Paul (Acts 9).

Philip the evangelist went down to Samaria and preached Christ to them (Acts 8). Although there is no mention of the resurrection, it is very obvious that he didn't miss this important fact out. Similarly with the divine connection with the eunuch—a man of great authority from Ethiopia—the Spirit of the Lord gave him specific instructions as to where he would meet this man. Philip was to get into the man's chariot; and as he did, the eunuch was actually reading from the prophecy of Isaiah.

Philip again preached Jesus to him; the eunuch believed and was baptized. You can't preach Jesus without the resurrection; this would be an integral part of Philip's message. Sometimes, we can read the accounts of these divine connections and think that they are limited to the book of the Acts of the Apostles, but the Holy Spirit is constantly searching for sinners and longing for us to listen more to His voice and directions. As we do, I am sure we will see divine connections which will lead to people surrendering their lives to Jesus Christ.

Peter had a similar experience through a vision he received at the same time the Holy Spirit was speaking to a man called Cornelius who was a centurion of the Italian Regiment. This man prayed and gave generously and God heard his prayers, but he needed to come to a saving knowledge of Jesus Christ. He is instructed as to where to send two of his household servants to find Peter; at the same time, Peter is receiving a revelation from God that this Gospel is for the Gentiles (non-Jews) as well as the Jews.

Peter travels to the house of Cornelius and preaches Christ to them, affirming the fact that He was raised from the dead. As he preached, the Holy Spirit came upon the whole household and they began to speak in tongues as did the believers on the day of Pentecost. Through a divine connection, the whole household was saved, baptized in water, and filled with the Holy Spirit (Acts 10). May God give us listening hearts and many Divine connections!

When Paul and his missionary party went to Thessalonica, they visited the synagogue of the Jews. He reasoned with them from the scriptures and preached the resurrection of Christ (Acts 17:1–2). It is interesting to note that Paul and his missionary party were only there for three Sabbath days, but many believed and they left a church behind!

The scripture tells us that a great multitude of devout Greeks believed along with some of the leading women. As with all revivals, there was a stirring up by the enemy of souls in unbelieving hearts and persecution broke out. Revival and persecution seem to go together. The reason is simple: it is a clash of two kingdoms—light and darkness, good and evil, the Kingdom of God and the power of darkness. Paul was no stranger to this as it had become part of the course, but then he knew all too well the reality of working for the wrong kingdom and had been the instigator of great persecution.

The Lord had made clear to him at his conversion that he was to suffer many things for the Gospel's sake. Despite all these happenings, the amazing thing is, after only three Sabbath days, he left a church behind and this became a church that he only had praise for and that went on to spread the Gospel to the whole area. The key to this is found in 1 Thessalonians 1:5: "For our gospel did not come to you in word only but also in power, and in the Holy Spirit and in much assurance as you know what kind of men we were among you for your sake."

The message of the resurrection came in the power of the Holy Spirit and with the kind of commitment that left the hearers in no doubt as to the conviction and passion of these servants of God. In fact, they were known as men who had turned the world upside down (Acts 17:6). The message of the resurrection always brings challenge and demands a decision.

At every opportunity, the apostles witnessed to the resurrection. When Paul stood before King Agrippa as a prisoner, he testified to the resurrection of Christ (Acts 26:23). And the book of the Acts of the Apostles ends with Paul under house arrest, and for two years, he continued to preach about the Kingdom of God and teach the things which concern the Lord Jesus Christ.

The message of the cross must always be backed up by the message of an empty tomb and a resurrected Christ.

The truth that Jesus died and rose again is a fact of history, and it would stand in any court of law. He was actually seen by five hundred and seventeen eyewitnesses during the forty-day period before He ascended to heaven. There are many theories that have been propagated to seek to disprove the resurrection, but none of them can stand against the truth.

One theory is that he only swooned on the cross that he wasn't actually dead; and when He was laid in the tomb, the cold air of the tomb revived Him. Imagine that to be true for a moment after all he had endured upon the cross to appear to His disciples three days later in perfect health and vitality. This would have been impossible!

Another theory suggests that His disciples stole the body. For that to actually happen, they would have had to pass by Roman guards who were under specific instructions to guard the tomb with their lives. There would have been no guards sleeping on the job during those three days and nights!

Another theory was that it was a projection of the minds of the disciples that they were so anticipating His resurrection they conjured it up in their minds. This could not have been the case because the Bible specifically says, "They didn't know the scripture that he would rise from the dead" (John 20:9). This simply means that although Jesus had told them of resurrection on a number of occasions, they had not really believed this. There had been no revelation in their hearts. After His death, they were left hopeless, afraid, and depressed. The two who walked the Emmaus road speaking of what had happened were discouraged until the risen Christ appeared to them walking by their side (Luke 24).

If the whole thing were a hoax, then the question must be asked, Why did this group of believers go on to risk their lives and some laid down their lives to spread the Gospel?

To return to Paul's argument and defense of the resurrection, if there is no resurrection, then Christ is not risen. If Christ is not risen, then our preaching is empty and so is our faith. That would make us false witnesses, and we would still be in our sins. Those believers already dead would have perished, and we would be the most miserable people around (1 Cor. 15:13–19).

The Gospel we preach declares, "But now Christ is risen from the dead, and has become the first fruits of those who have died" (1 Cor. 15:20).

The resurrection of Jesus Christ was a bodily resurrection. When He appeared to His disciples, He said, "A spirit does not have flesh and bone as you see I have" (Luke 24:39). It may be hard for us to understand that a tangible body that could be handled and touched as He invited Thomas to do, in order to erase any trace of doubt from his mind, could enter a room and appear and disappear. Yet He wasn't a spirit! He could also eat and drink; it was Jesus in resurrection form that invited Peter to join Him for breakfast on the shores of Galilee after Peter and some of the disciples had been fishing all night and caught nothing (John 21).

Jesus was in His resurrection the first fruits or the forerunner. His resurrection is the pattern for the believer's resurrection. Paul addresses the questions of what kind of body will believers have in the resurrection and how they will be raised (1 Cor. 15:35). Paul uses a simple illustration of sowing seed. The seed has to die to germinate, and the seed that is sown does not appear as a seed when breaking through the soil but, rather, the body of the plant appears. When it appears, it is not identical to the seed that was sown. He also illustrates the differences of animal flesh, fish, and birds; they all have their different kinds of flesh and so does man. He goes on to state that in God's creative genius there is variety in the universe, that even stars are different the one from the other (1 Cor. 15:41).

When we consider what Paul is teaching, it doesn't matter how long a person has been dead or what kind of death they died, whether they were maimed burnt lost at sea blown up in war or suffered amputations. God doesn't need a whole body to bring about resurrection; He just uses the seed. The body that will be raised will not be identical to the one that died, but it will be changed, and there will be individuality as there is now. As to the question *Will we know each other in heaven?* the answer has to be a definite *yes.* How could heaven be far better if we were all strangers? One day, we shall know even as we are known; our knowledge is limited here, but in heaven it will be perfected (1 Cor. 13).

As mentioned in this book, our life is in our blood, but the resurrection body will not have blood—it will be filled with the life of God. This new body will not grow old, never die, and never get sick. There will be no medical bills in heaven or insurance premiums, no hospitals, or need for physical checkups. In our earthly life, we bore the image of the man (Adam) made from dust, but in the resurrection we shall bear the image of the heavenly man. The apostle John wrote, "When He shall appear we shall be like Him for we shall see Him as He is" (1 John 3:2).

One day, a trumpet will sound from the throne room of heaven. Trumpets were used in various ways in the Old Testament—sometimes to summon the tribes of Israel to gather, other times to mark some feast or celebration day, and they also used the trumpet to gather the troops to battle. A trumpet will sound one day that will mark the return of the Lord Jesus Christ. On that day, those believers who are alive at His coming will be changed in the twinkling of an eye. Changed in the sense that mortality will be changed to immortality, and at the same time, the dead bodies of believers will be raised from their graves in resurrection life to be united with their spirit that has been in the presence of the Lord.

Graves will be emptied; death will be finally defeated and swallowed up in victory. Death still has a sting and still seems to have a victory. It leaves broken hearts, empty chairs, a widow or widower feeling desolate, and the family circle broken.

Shortly after the events of September 11, 2001, when the twin towers fell in New York, Queen Elizabeth sent a letter to President Bush in which she expressed her deep sorrow for the loss of so many lives. She also wrote this line: "Grief is the price we pay for having loved." One day, there will be no more grief, no more tears, and no more death.

Resurrection—this is the Gospel we preach.

10

The Gospel That Delivers
from Judgment

The Gospel of God's grace and love is preeminent today in most preaching and, of course, should always be at the heart of the Gospel. The well-known verse in John 3:16, "For God so loved the world that he gave His only begotten Son that whoever believes in Him should not perish but have everlasting life," is the Gospel message. But we also need to take note of the last line of that verse: "Shall not perish but have everlasting life."

This presents us with two extremes. On the one hand is the everlasting life that comes from believing in the Son of God, and on the other, the fate of the unbeliever is that they will perish. It is this fact that is unpopular, that is disturbing, and that many find difficult to come to terms with—that a God of love could also be a God of judgment.

As stated in previous chapters, the truth is that God is governed by His character, so a God of love will always forgive the repentant sinner. But I must emphasize that the sinner has to repent to gain forgiveness. The fact also that God is holy means He cannot overlook sin, and again I make the point that is what the cross is all about. That is where God's judgment was poured out. Jesus took the judgment of God's wrath against sin upon Himself and suffered and died in our place (Isa. 53:4–5).

It is difficult to ignore that fact that God does display His wrath and judgment at times. To read through the Old Testament, one cannot ignore the many times when He, because of Israel's disobedience and sin, poured out judgment. God is glorified in both revival and judgment when He has first given His word.

The prophets of the Old Testament warned of coming judgment for the sins of the nations. Israel and Judah were taken into captivity. Even in the wilderness, Israel tasted the judgment of God with fiery serpents, bringing death to thousands, until Moses interceded and made a brass serpent. The answer, as already stated in a previous chapter, was that anyone bitten would simply have to look at the brass serpent in order to be healed and live. Think about Sodom and Gomorrah.

Because of the people's total depravity and abominable sin, God rained fire and brimstone upon the cities and destroyed them (Gen. 19). Don't forget, also in Noah's day, the whole earth was flooded with the waters of God's judgment. The world perished in the flood apart from Noah's immediate family and his son's wives along with the animals that were in the ark. This again was because of gross sin in the earth and a total unconcern for God.

If that sounds difficult to believe, remember, Jesus actually put the stamp mark of truth upon this by saying, "As it was in the days of Noah so shall it be in the days of the coming of the Son of man" (Matt. 24:37). He went on to say that at the time of this judgment, the people were eating and drinking, marrying and giving in marriage until the day that Noah entered the ark (Matt. 24:37–38). In other words, there was a total unconcern for Noah's warning message and they just continued on as normal. But the day dawned when it was not normal anymore, rain came from heaven and waters gushed up from beneath the earth, and the judgment of God came after the world (that then was) had refused to repent! It is important to point out that God's judgment came upon the world after "the longsuffering of God waited in the days of Noah, while the ark was being prepared, in which few souls that is eight souls were saved through water" (1 Peter 3:20).

Noah was five hundred years old when he received directions from God to build the ark, and he was six hundred years old when he entered into the ark. For one hundred years, Noah preached righteousness and warned of coming judgment!

When children in Sunday school are taught about Noah and the ark, we often see their drawings and paintings of the animals walking into the ark two by two. Of course, we wouldn't want them to particularly draw angry waves and thousands of people drowning, but that is exactly what happened!

God's judgment came upon idolatrous nations as Israel took control of the promised land of Canaan. Some may say, "But that is all Old Testament. Surely, God is no longer dealing in judgment."

First of all, the fact that He has poured out judgment means that He reserves the right to do so. Second, if God has done this, then it must be in keeping with His character.

Paul, when writing to the Thessalonians in 1 Thessalonians 1:7–9 regarding the coming of the Lord, says that He will be "revealed from heaven with His mighty angels, in flaming fire taking vengeance on those who do not obey the Gospel of our Lord Jesus Christ. These shall be punished with everlasting destruction from the presence of the Lord and from the glory of His power."

The very last book in the Bible, the book of the Revelation of Jesus Christ, shows the church's ultimate triumph, the God of the ages intervening in the world, and the glories of heaven that awaits those who are redeemed and saved. But it also depicts quite clearly the end-time judgments of God that will be poured out on the world.

Consider just one of the chapters in the book of the Revelation, Revelation 13. It describes a third of mankind will be killed by the smoke and brimstone that will come upon the world and four angels that will be released to bring this judgment (Rev. 13:15).

The fascinating thing is this, that despite all this judgment, the Bible says

But the rest of mankind who were not killed by these plagues did not repent of the works of their hands, that they should not worship demons, and idols of gold, silver, brass, stone, and wood which can neither see nor hear nor walk. And they did not repent of their murders or their sorceries or their sexual immorality or their thefts. (Rev. 9:20–21)

This shows us the great deception that the devil brings upon the minds of people and the hardness of the human heart that is given over to sin.

The book of the Revelation also depicts what is called the "Great White Throne Judgment" (Rev. 20:11–15). These verses describe the dead, both small and great, standing before God. Whatever their social standing was, whether they have had the accolades of men or whether they had passed through the world barely noticed—the rich and the poor, high class and lower class, and presidents and monarchs—if their names are not written in the Book of Life, they will all stand side by side. Wealth and riches or worldly power will no longer count on that day when the Book is opened. Everything will have been logged in the Book; but if their name is not written in the book of life, they will be cast into the lake of fire!

These verses never made the "old promise box." I remember seeing people take a tiny, little scroll of paper from their promise box. It was filled with wonderful promises of God's goodness and amazing promises, but there was never anything of judgment in those boxes and, rightly so, because they were designed to encourage believers with God's promises. The book of the Revelation does both. It encourages believers that the final triumph is in the hands of God and the church—God's masterpiece—will one day be partakers of all that He has prepared in eternity and will ultimately understand what it really means to be heirs of the Father and joint heirs with the Son.

But it also serves as a solemn reminder of the judgment of God that awaits the unbeliever.

This, as already stated, is a solemn truth that is often avoided in modern preaching. The consideration of this truth should produce a greater reverence for the Lord and His salvation and a greater urgency to reach the unbeliever with the message of the Gospel of Grace. The questions we must ask are questions like the following:

- Can we trust the words of Jesus?
- Should we be the decider of what is truth and what is fiction?
- Did He say things just to scare people into believing?
- If we dismiss His teaching on hell, then are we to dismiss His teachings on heaven?
- Why is it that at the great "White Throne Judgment" described in the book of the Revelation are the dead raised with physical bodies?
- Where does the disembodied spirit go after death?
- Is hell an eternal punishment?
- What is hell really like?

Jesus declared Himself to be the Way, the Truth, and the Life; He also proved Himself to be the Son of God by His resurrection from the dead. His resurrection sealed everything He had said and every promise He had made. His words of eternal life and His words of eternal damnation cannot be separated if He is the Truth! However, the human mind either wants to rule out God altogether and simply believe that there is no life after death. Or it wants to make God into a someone who so loved the world that He gave His only Son in order to die upon the cross for our sins but it really doesn't matter too much about the cross because, in the end, everyone will get to heaven (or, at least, those who have tried to do their best)!

To ponder that first thought for a moment, which would suggest there is no life after death, is quite depressing—to imagine that when one gets to old age, there is nothing to look forward to, only memories to look back upon that will soon be erased forever. In a recent ministry trip to Madagascar, my wife and I were having a meal in the hotel restaurant, and a gentleman came over to speak to us on hearing our English accent. He had been dining alone, so we asked him to join us.

During our conversation, we learned he was from Switzerland working for one year in Madagascar. His marriage had ended some years ago, his daughters lived in other countries, and he seemed quite lonely. We also discovered he was an atheist! We were able to share the Gospel with him and assured him we would be praying for him. As we parted company that night, the thought just struck home again to me that the atheist has nothing to look forward to. As quoted in the previous chapter, the apostle Paul declared that if we have hope only in Christ in this world, we are of all men most miserable (1 Cor. 15:19)!

Jesus didn't speak of Hell with the intention of frightening people but, rather, warning them. If a house was about to blow up with explosives and you had prior knowledge, you wouldn't share that with the sole intention of frightening people; your motive would be for them to escape from the scene unharmed!

Our definition of *love* is often colored by sentimentalism. Surely, if we can forgive someone, then how much more should God? However, God is not filled with sentimentalism but with genuine love that will not allow anything to spoil again what He has in store and prepared for those who love Him. We would never consider putting a child molester in a dormitory with small children, right? Love for those children would protect them from such an unthinkable act; and at the same time, we would bolt the door so no outside intrusion would be possible. The Lord has made heaven accessible through His cross, but first there has to be a heart transformation by believing the Gospel and repentance from sin.

Now, let me try and shed some light and understanding on some of the terms used in the Bible such as *Sheol, Hades, Tartarus,* and *Gehenna*

Several different Greek words for hell are used in the New Testament.

Tartarus

Tartarus is found in 2 Peter 2:4 and Jude 1:6. Both these scriptures are referring to the time of Noah. Sin had corrupted the human race; and as early as Eden after the fall of man, it was stated that Cain, who killed his brother Abel, was "of that wicked one" (1 John 3:12). The onslaught on the human race had begun, and we little realize the utter depravity that was taking place upon the earth.

Take note of the passage in 2 Peter 2:4–5:

> God spared not the angels that sinned but cast them down to *Tartarus* [italics mine] and delivered them into chains of darkness to be reserved unto judgment, and spared not the old world but saved Noah.

The rebellion that had taken place in heaven by Satan, whose heart had become lifted up with pride, was such that other angels rebelled with him (Isa. 14:12–14). Some of these angels appear to have already been banished to eternal punishment. The question is, What had these angels done that caused God to banish them to eternal judgment?

There are some scriptures that seem difficult to be emphatic about, one of which is "the sons of God went into the daughters of men and there were giants in the earth!" (Gen. 6:4).

Could this be a reference to the fact that these rebellious angels had possessed the daughters of men and the result was that their offspring were like giants? Was the population of the earth in danger of becoming possessed by demons? Whatever we may think, the truth is that the earth had become so corrupt that God had to flood the earth and destroy the human race, apart from Noah and his immediate family as an act of love and to keep His plans and purposes on track.

Whatever was happening on the earth at that time was utter corruption and an abomination in God's sight. God doesn't pour out that kind of judgment at a moment's notice. The world had been warned for one hundred years. But after God had patiently waited with longsuffering, His judgments broke forth as the bowels of the earth gushed forth water and the heavens opened with unstoppable deluges until the earth was once again covered in water!

It also seems that the demons that were allowed to roam at this time understood that their time of judgment would come. When Jesus was about to cast them out of the demoniac, they begged Him not to torment them before their time (Matt. 8:29).

Tartarus is a place distinct from Hades or Hell. It is like a dungeon, a place of confinement (2 Pet. 2:4). The rebellious angels will one day be with the devil in the lake of fire and experience eternal everlasting punishment.

Gehenna

Gehenna is another word used which describes what hell is like. *Gehenna* means the "valley of Hinnom." In Israel's history, it was the place were infant sacrifices, idolatries, and infidelities took place (Josh. 15:8; 2 Kings 23:10; Neh. 11:30).

The Jews gave human sacrifices to pagan deities in that very valley outside of Jerusalem. It was also a garbage dump which bred worms where the fire never went out. Jesus referred to hell as a place "where their worm does not die and fire is not quenched" (Mark 9:44, 46, 48).

Hades

Hades is a word in the New Testament that has been translated from the word *Sheol*. They are basically the same as stated in Psalm 16:10: "For you will not leave my soul in hell [Sheol], neither will you suffer your holy one to see corruption."

The word *Sheol* is translated "Hades," or hell, in Acts 2:27; and Peter is quoting from Psalm 16.

Sheol is the Old testament name for the place of departed souls corresponding to the New Testament word Hades. The word occurs 65 times in the Hebrew Old Testament and is rendered in the KJV 31 times grave and 3 times pit. The reason for the variety of translation is that hell is ordinarily thought of as a place of punishment and so grave is substituted when the reference is to the souls of good men, e.g. Jacob said that he would go down into the grave mourning for his son (Genesis 37:35). Quote taken from the Zondervan Bible dictionary.

Sheol, or Hades, seems to have had two compartments, which is verified with Jesus's teaching of the story of the rich man and Lazarus in Luke 16:23–26.

The story speaks of both men dying and going to different places—one was in torment, the other in what is described as "Abraham's bosom," or a place of rest and security and peace. This must not be interpreted as though it was because one was rich he went to Hades and because the other was poor he went to Abraham's bosom, the truth we need to understand is that between the two places was a gulf fixed and neither could cross over to the other. The whole point of the story was to depict the utter extremes of torment and peace and that in the lifetime of the rich man, he had taken no notice of what the Prophets had said and the scriptures declared. Neither had he sought at all to help poor Lazarus who had been laid at his gate, daily dying from his sores. Remember, the rich man was in great torment and distress, and he was still only in Hades this is not the final judgment the lake of fire referred to in (Revelation 20:11-15).

After Christ's ascension, believers go directly to heaven; prior to this, believers were in Hades, or "Abraham's bosom." On the cross, Jesus promised the repentant thief that on that very day he would be with Him in Paradise.

It seems that when Jesus died before His resurrection took place, He went into Hades and led all those who had been waiting to be taken to heaven in a triumphal procession into the place that had been prepared for them called paradise.

The word *paradise* is found only three times in the New Testament, specifically in *Luke 23:43, 2 Corinthians 12:4*, and *Revelation 2:7*. The apostle Paul refers to paradise as the third heaven.

We do well to remember, when considering the subject of hell, that it was never intended for any others except the devil and his angels. Such was their rebellion. However, when we consider the scene set in the book of the Revelation, when the dead—small and great—stand before God and the books are opened, anyone whose name is not written in the Book of Life is to be cast into the lake of fire. This is the same judgment that the devil and his angels receive.

It may surprise you that the devil is not in hell yet! At the Great White Throne Judgment, when the dead small and great stand before God, they will not stand before Him as disembodied spirits but with bodies as in their earthly life.

If that is not sufficient to turn anyone away from a life of unbelief and sin, think about the phrase that says their torment will be "forever and ever" (Rev. 20:10).

Consider other scriptures that speak of "everlasting punishment":

- "Everlasting fire" (Matt. 25:41).
- "Everlasting punishment" (Matt. 25:46).
- "Eternal damnation" (Mark 6:29)
- "Everlasting destruction" (2 Thess. 1:9).

The words used for *everlasting life* is found in John 3:16 and *everlasting God* in Romans 16:26.

The word *everlasting* ("aionios") is derived from the word *aion* signifying an age or duration. The scripture speaks of two ages, the present and the one to come. The present refers to this world and is temporal and contrasted with the age to come, which is endless. It seems that in every scripture where the word *aionios* is used for the future punishment of the unbeliever, it denotes endless duration.

The study of eternal punishment and its preaching may not be popular, but we must always come back to the horrors of the cross and recognize that Jesus went through hell while hanging on the cross. He received the judgment and billows of God's wrath and, for the first time in all eternity, was separated from God. To be separated from God is hell. No wonder the sky turned black as all hell poured its onslaught upon the Son of God. If there was no hell and no judgment, then why was the cross planned from the foundation of the world? Why was it necessary for the crucifixion of the Son of God?

The Gospel delivers from the judgment of God and the eternal punishment of a hell which was created for the devil and his angels.

This the Gospel we preach.

11

Heaven

We now turn to a happier theme that is of heaven. The scripture leaves us in no doubt as to the validity of heaven. The book of the Revelation describes multitudes worshiping God in heaven. In fact, in this same book, we have described heaven in many positive ways; and it also tells us some of the things that will not be in heaven, which we will look at later in this chapter.

Many people who are prone to believe in heaven would have difficulty believing in hell. In fact, as we have written in earlier chapters, the common belief of one day making it to heaven is dependent on the individual having lived a good enough life.

Imagine for a moment you see a wonderful mansion set in acres of its own grounds, and you would really like to live there. So, one day, you walk up to the front door and ring the doorbell. The owner comes to the door and you express to him that you are a good citizen and you have never been in any kind of trouble with the law and the reason you are there is that you would like to live in his house. What do you think his response would be? Why would he let you live there even if you have lived an exemplary life? His answer would simply be "I don't know you, it is only my family who live here." Access to his home is on the basis of relationship only. Access into heaven is exactly the same—it is on the basis of whether we have come to know the Lord Jesus Christ.

The apostle Paul, when writing to the Corinthian Church, wrote of knowing a man who was caught up into the third heaven, which he describes as paradise, and he heard inexpressible things—things that man was not permitted to tell (2 Cor. 12:1–4).

Jesus promised the repentant thief on the cross that he would be with Him in paradise that very day. It is obvious then that when the believer dies, there is not a waiting period before the soul reaches heaven and neither is there a holding place until certain sins have been atoned for. The Bible does not teach that, but rather, atonement was made at the cross and, through faith in Christ, the believer is declared righteous.

To continue the thought of immediate entry into heaven at death for the believer, the apostle Paul declared that he was torn between the two. On one hand, his ministry would lead to more fruitfulness and blessing to the churches, but on the other hand, to die would be gain to him (Phil. 1:21–26). When Paul wrote this letter, he was under house arrest, chained to a soldier; yet in no way was he doubting despite his hardships and persecution.

His faith shone through the darkest of situations and the most severe trials and in verse 23, he declared that to depart and to be with Christ is far better.

Paul was actually saying that heaven is far superior to this world and to be with Christ is far better than living in this world. We can only imagine what heaven is really like, but to imagine something far better is definitely in keeping with the way God works. He always keeps the best for the last!

It was the best wine that came forth when Jesus changed water into wine at the wedding in Cana of Galilee. Even the governor of the feast testified to that. Jesus always keeps the best for the last. In that way, there is always the element of excitement, surprise, and anticipation. I am not of the persuasion, as some are, that the last days will be all doom and gloom. I believe in the world. Things will get worse as Paul described to Timothy when writing of the last days. But in the church, we have the promise in the last days God will pour out His Spirit and supernatural things will happen. As men's hearts fail them for fear in the last days, the greatest harvest of souls will take place and the demonstrations of God's glory will be seen as the church is seen to rise and shine.

When I was a child, I well remember the excitement of Christmas Day, there was always one special present I really wanted. I could generally tell which that was without unwrapping it, so I would unwrap all the others and leave the special one to the last as this was the best. The apostle Paul viewed heaven in much the same way when he described it as far better.

To follow this thought through, we would have to say that if heaven is far better, then we definitely are not in a "soul sleep" as some would teach. There were occasions when Jesus used this term *sleeping* when referring to death, one of which is when He heard that Lazarus had become sick. "Lazarus has fallen asleep, but I am going to wake him up" (John 11:11). We then read in verses 14, Jesus told His disciples plainly that Lazarus is dead.

The word *sleep* when used in connection with death is simply referring to the body being in a similar state of that when someone is sleeping. Nowhere in the scripture do we have any teaching that the souls of the dead are sleeping waiting for the day of resurrection. On the contrary, when we have insight from scripture of those who have died, it always speaks of consciousness. Neither the beggar who went into Abraham's bosom or the rich man who lifted up his eyes in torment was asleep but, rather, very much awake and alert as to where they were.

If we all fell into an unconscious sleep at the moment of death, how could that be described as being far better? The apostle Paul actually used the word *desire* when referring to the thought of going to be with Christ (Phil. 1:23). Also notice that when Paul uses the word *depart*, it is followed with the phrase "to be with Christ." When writing to the Corinthian Church, especially in 2 Corinthians 5:6–9, Paul declares that to be absent from the body is to be present with the Lord and also that he would prefer to be absent from the body in order to be present with the Lord.

As a boy in school, the teacher would call the register at the beginning of the first class each morning. Those who were in class would be marked as present and those who were not as absent. When you look upon the dead body of an individual, you are seeing their earthly house in which their soul and spirit had once resided but which are now absent. The moment the believer is absent from the body, he or she is present with the Lord. The last breath on earth is followed by the next in heaven. A spoiled and soiled, old world is exchanged for the delights and surprises of heaven.

Paul uses the word *depart*, which A.T. Robertson translates as "loosing anchor and putting out to sea." It was said of Smith Wigglesworth, who was called the "Apostle of Faith," that when he died, his departure must have resembled a fully laden ship leaving harbor. Such was the faith and supernatural gifts that he moved in during his ministry.

One day, our anchor to this world will be lifted, and none of us know when but believers can be prepared and assured of our destination. The other description Paul uses is that of the human body being like a tent: "We know that if this earthly tent we live in is destroyed we have a building from God an eternal house in the heavens not built by human hands" (2 Cor. 5:1).

When our boys were much younger, we would go camping. We had what was called a trailer tent. It was fairly easy to erect as we would hitch it up on the back of the car and off we would go. The tent part would simply pull out onto the wooden base, and within a fairly short space of time, we would have everything erect. Of course, tents are fine when the weather is good and the wind doesn't blow too hard, but when it's wet and windy it's not much fun. I well remember being on such a holiday and waking up to a damp, rainy day and thinking, *Are we supposed to be enjoying this?* After a few days, we decided we would pack everything up and go and spend the rest of the time with my parents. I think that was the last time we went camping!

Tents can easily tear, and they are flimsy compared with bricks and mortar. Our bodies are compared to earthly tents—they are not going to last forever and they can get sick—but in this life, it is this earthly tent where our soul and spirit reside. What awaits us in heaven is an exchange. We absent our earthly tent and move to a house not made with hands (2 Cor. 5:1–4). Keep in mind the first verse: "For we know that if the earthly tent we live in is dissolved we have a building of God an house not made with hands or an eternal body made for us by God Himself."

Notice also that Paul goes on to say that "we desire to be clothed upon with our new body" (2 Cor. 5:4). This leads us to the thought that awaiting the believer is a new body once they arrive in heaven. This may well be exchanged one day at the resurrection for a body like Christ's that He revealed to His disciples as a body with flesh and bones but was not a spirit. However, the Bible teaches that there seems to be a body that God prepares for the believer awaiting them in heaven. This would also seem to confirm the fact that when Jesus was transfigured on the mountain in front of Peter, James, and John, there appeared also Moses and Elijah. They also recognized them as such, which would answer the question as to whether we will know each other in heaven.

When one preacher was asked that question, his reply was "You don't think we will be bigger fools in heaven than what we are down here do you?" Would heaven be heaven if we didn't recognize loved ones and friends? Of course not. We will know even as we are known. Heaven will be the place of great reunions. Very often, when being at the airport, we have seen tears both in the departure lounge and arrival lounge. Tears of sorrow in one because loved ones or friends depart and tears of joy in the other because of reunions. In heaven, there will only be reunions.

One of my favorite verses regarding the state of the believer in heaven is found in 2 Corinthians 5:4: "For we that are in this tent groan being burdened not that we should be unclothed but clothed upon, that mortality might be swallowed up by life."

When the believer dies, they are swallowed up by life! They have never been more alive! The Lord Jesus Christ declared Himself to be the Way, the Truth, and the Life. At His raising of Lazarus, He declared Himself to be the resurrection and the life. He went on to say, "He that believes in Me though he were dead yet shall he live and he who lives and believes in Me shall never die" (John 11:25). Faith in Christ raises the sinner from spiritual death, and those who live and believe will never die!

The definition of *death* is "separation from the One who is the Life." Paul declared that nothing can separate the believer from the love of God in Christ Jesus, not even death itself (Romans 8:18). As Jonah was swallowed up by the great fish, the believer at death will be swallowed up by life. Imagine—every fiber of our being filled with the life of God! Think about those times when the presence of God has been so real, almost tangible; but to be swallowed up by life will surpass those greatest moments.

Even now, the believer knows and experiences a peace that passes understanding and joy that is unspeakable, but that will be nothing in comparison to what awaits the believer who is swallowed up by life. This is God's purpose, and He has given us the Holy Spirit as our guarantee so we are always confident as the apostle Paul says, "While we are at home in the body we are absent from the Lord" (2 Cor. 5:6). But he goes on later in scripture to say that "we are confident and willing rather to be absent from the body and present with the Lord" (2 Cor. 5:8).

We so often hear people say "I think so," "I may be wrong," or "I'm not sure." That is not the language Paul used. He was certain and confident. How could we have any joy without such confidence and assurance?

The book of the Revelation describes heaven by telling us a number of things that won't be there as we read from Revelation 21:1: "Now I saw a new heaven and a new earth, for the first heaven and the first earth had passed away and there was no more sea."

I have always loved being by the sea. In a recent ministry trip to a conference in Namibia, there was a young man who had traveled from Zambia. The country of Zambia is landlocked, and he had never seen the sea. He was overjoyed to actually be looking at the great Atlantic Ocean for the first time. At first thought, the fact that there will be no more oceans in heaven seems difficult to understand, but I'm sure God has His reasons and has something better. One of the problems with the oceans of the world is they separate people. It is one thing to live in the same country as your family and loved ones even though you may live miles apart, but it's another when you are separated by an ocean!

In heaven, there will be no separations either from the love of God or from our loved ones, family, and friends, no more seas. There will be no more tears in heaven or will there? "God will wipe away every tear from their eyes," as said in Revelation 21:4.

The psalmist says, "Return to your rest, O my soul, for the Lord has dealt bountifully with you. For you have delivered my soul from death, my eyes from tears and my feet from falling" (Ps. 116:7–8). Heaven will definitely be a place of rest, where the soul is without worries and cares; however, it will also be a place where God will wipe away every tear. It doesn't actually says "There will be no tears" but, rather, that God will wipe away every tear. It is just a thought, but maybe there will be some who will look back on their earthly life and perhaps wish they had served God better. If there are tears, even they will be wiped away by the love of God.

Somehow in God's love, compassion, and wisdom, He has the ability to wipe away anything that would mar our enjoyment of heaven. Sometimes. the question *What about friends or family members that will not be in heaven?* is asked. It would not be heaven if we lived in eternity with the sorrow of those who are lost. God has all of that taken care of in His grace and love, and there are some things we find difficult to comprehend in our earthly life. But one day, we will have full knowledge. "For we know in part and we prophesy in part, but when that which is perfect is come, then that which is in part will be done away," as we learn in 1 Corinthians 13:9–10). (The Living Bible renders those verses as, "Now our knowledge is partial and incomplete and even the gift of prophecy reveals only part of the whole picture. But when full understanding comes these partial things will become useless.")

In heaven, there will be no more death. Our new bodies will not decay, get sick, or grow old. There will be no more funerals, empty chairs, or lives left bereft of a life partner or family member. Death was never intended to be part of life. Even Jesus wept at the tomb of His friend Lazarus. It is still an enemy, but in heaven it will be no more.

There will be no more sorrow or crying and no more pain in heaven. The storms of life with all its sickness, disappointments, tragedies, and physical and emotional pain will be no more. Peace will reign supreme, for the Prince of Peace will be seated on the throne. All those former things that we have battled with will be done away. No wonder Paul said, "It is far better to be with Christ" (Phil. 1:23).

The New Jerusalem is described in Revelation 21; all of its glory and splendor await the redeemed of the Lord. His glory will be the light there will be no more need for sun or the moon; the Lamb is its light (Rev. 21:23). The glory of God that came shining through as Jesus was transfigured before Peter, James, and John will be the glory that will light up the New Jerusalem. There will be nothing allowed to enter that would defile or cause abomination or even a lie but only those whose names are written in the Lamb's Book of Life (Rev. 21:27).

In Revelation 22, we have described a "pure river of water of life" clear as crystal proceeding from the throne of God and of the Lamb. Jesus promised the woman at the well that He could give her "living water" and she would never thirst again if she asked Him for it. Here we find the water of life coming from the throne. Everything about heaven speaks of life light, joy, peace, tranquility, and God's provision and presence for His redeemed people.

One other thing that is worthy of note is that the New Jerusalem will have a street of gold like transparent glass (Rev. 21:21). In this world, men give their lives for gold, for the "American dream," and for riches and wealth. We are constantly being told on TV to put our money into gold. Isn't it amazing that, one day what men have lived and worked for, we will actually be walking on it?

The Lord has spared nothing for our enjoyment when it comes to heaven. Jesus told His disciples (John 14) that He was to go to prepare a place for them and one day He would return to take His church back to the place He had prepared. The Lord created this world in six days. If He has been working on preparing heaven for over two thousand years, we are in for some exciting things. Just a thought!

Always remember that Jesus declared to the Sadducees that God is the God of Abraham, Isaac, and Jacob; and He is not the God of the dead but of the living (Matt. 22:32). If you have gone through the grief of losing a loved one, if that loved one is a believer, be assured they are not lost. To lose someone means we don't know where they are. As believers, we certainly do know exactly where they are. One other thought is that sometimes parents may say they used to have two children but one unfortunately died. The truth is, although one died, they still are the parents of two children because the one who has gone to heaven is very much alive. My parents had a child before I was born; he lived to be a few months old. I have always thought of myself as an only child until I realized the truth of Matthew 22:32. The truth is, I have a brother who I have never met but one day we will meet on heaven's shore.

The old hymn says it all: "What a gathering, what a gathering what a gathering of the ransomed in the summer land of love, what a gathering what a gathering of the ransomed in that happy home above."

Our loved ones who have gone on to heaven before us are not just in our past, but they are definitely in our future. Heaven is far better.

This is the Gospel we preach.

12

The Gospel of Power

Who better to write about the Gospel of power than the apostle Paul? He had been the greatest enemy of the church until he was converted. Saul of Tarsus became better known after his conversion as the apostle Paul.

When writing to the church at Rome, he testified to his belief in "the Gospel of Power" when he wrote, "I am not ashamed of the Gospel of Christ for it is the power of God unto salvation for everyone who believes, for the Jew first and also for the Greek" (Rom. 1:16).

He opens the first chapter of Romans 1 by calling himself a "bondservant of Jesus Christ." Freely, willingly, Paul felt privileged to call himself that. After all that Christ had done for him, it was only reasonable, in Paul's eyes, that he should give everything he could back to the One who had saved him and forgiven him. He introduces Jesus Christ as the One who was declared to be the Son of God with power according to the Spirit of holiness by the resurrection from the dead (Rom. 1:4).

Paul had never visited Rome but longed to do so. The gospel Paul preached was for all nations, including the might and power of Rome. Known for its military might and the power of the sword, Paul calls the gospel the "Power of God unto salvation." A greater power was at work; and it had nothing to do with military power or earthly weapons but, rather, the power of God that worked through the preaching of the Gospel.

It was this power and this gospel that of which Paul was not ashamed; it was this gospel that had completely revolutionized his life. The transformation of his conversion was even hard for some of the early disciples to believe when they first heard the news. As time went on, it was plain to see that what had happened to Paul was not some mere fad but an encounter with God that left him completely changed. Of this gospel, Paul was not ashamed, he was not embarrassed he didn't blush; this Gospel was worth living and dying for if necessary. Paul had freely laid himself upon the altar of sacrifice and felt in debt to all men (v. 14). He felt obligated also to take this message to the Jews first; after all, they were the nation who had been granted all the privileges of God's covenant promises. Their history was one of which God had chosen them, called them, and set them apart. Jesus Himself was born a Jew, and yet it was the Jews who turned against Him and in so doing missed the time of their visitation. The religious hierarchy was happy to see the Nazarene hounded to the cross and happy also to let the Romans crucify Him.

Crucifixion didn't end the story resurrection changed everything!

To understand some of the depths of this statement that the Gospel of Christ is the power of God unto salvation, we need to understand the total depravity of the human heart in these scriptures:

- "The heart is deceitful above all things and desperately wicked" (Jer. 17:9).
- "There is none that does good no not one" (Rom. 3:11–12).

Although the Bible says "There is none that does good," it doesn't actually mean that no one does good but, rather, that we cannot do anything good enough to satisfy God. Unconverted people are also responsible for many good things like acts of charity, self-sacrifice, and many commendable things in response to the needs of the world. But none of these things can actually satisfy God in the sense of bringing people into a relationship with Him. There is only One who could do that, and it was the One who gave Himself as a sinless sacrifice upon the cross and became the "propitiation for our sins."

The very heart or core of man's being is, as the Bible says, "deceitful and desperately wicked." When Adam sinned, it was not something that was simply a mistake that could be rectified with better behavior but, rather, sin that affected him in such a way that he could never regain the position he had lost without the grace of God providing a perfect sacrifice. Sin disconnected Adam to his life source. His spirit died within him; yet at the same time, he was still operating with a physical body and a soul, the soul being the seat of our emotions our will and intellect.

Although spiritually dead as we learn in the Bible in Genesis 2:17—"In the day you eat of the tree of the knowledge of good and evil, in that day you will surely die"—Adam was still alive and had the capacity to choose, he still had a free will. He died spiritually in the sense that his spirit was now disconnected from God. Separation from God is really the definition of death. He did not lose the capacity to make choices. The total depravity of man is the fact that man is spiritually dead in sins (Eph. 2:1), but this does not mean that he cannot do anything for himself to regain the position that Adam lost. The spiritually dead person has not had free will and the ability to choose taken from him. When the Gospel is preached and the message of salvation is made clear, the spiritually dead man or woman has the ability to make a choice to surrender to Christ or to dismiss the message.

If a lightbulb is disconnected from its socket, it is still a lightbulb though there is no light. The only way it will give light is when it is reconnected. It is the same with the sinner who needs to be reconnected with God; the only difference in this illustration is the light bulb is completely helpless to make the decision to be reconnected. The sinner does have the ability to make the choice as to whether he or she remains in a lost condition disconnected from God or to turn in repentance and faith to our only hope and Savior Jesus Christ.

When Adam sinned, he still had a conscience—that is, he still had the ability to know what was morally right and wrong. The problem was that after Adam had become disconnected from God, his fallen state of sin did not allow him the power to use them right. He found himself with a nature that was fallen, the power of sin working within him. His thoughts became darkened and his desires were for self-gratification. There was a power working within him that crippled him and held him earthbound, deceived him, and stole his desires for God's presence. He became the servant of sin, not righteousness (Rom. 6:20).

James asks the question "Where do wars and fights come from among you? Don't they come from your desires for pleasure that war in your members?" (James 4:1). Adam found himself with an inner war that was now working with in him that dictated the way how he acted and thought. It was the power of sin. When Paul writes to the church at Rome (Rom. 8), he contrasts the flesh or our selfish, carnal ways against the spirit. Remember, Paul is writing to believers who had discovered the power of God's salvation, yet he is clearly teaching that they must make sure they live in accordance with the Spirit who had brought them back into relationship with God. It is possible then that believers can slip into selfish, carnal ways because of a sin nature working within them.

What we set our minds upon determines our behavior. To be spiritually minded is life and peace but to be carnally minded is death. The carnal mind is enmity against God for it is not subject to the law of God and cannot be. It is completely divorced from the life of God; it doesn't want to think on the things of God. This is the power of sin and the sin nature. There is no way that we can please God by operating in the carnal nature (Rom. 8:5–8). This carnal nature called "the flesh's lusts against the Spirit" is contrary to the Spirit; and if the believer does not walk in the Spirit or feed the spiritual life and renew the mind, then the old nature or flesh will surface. It is ugly when it does. It takes away the peace of God and manifests itself in things like adultery, fornication, uncleanness, lewdness idolatry, sorcery, hatred, contentions, jealousies, outbursts of wrath, selfish ambitions, dissensions, heresies, envies, murders, drunkenness, revelries, and the like (Gal. 5:16–21).

The selfish, carnal nature immediately took over once Adam had sinned. Fear took over from faith. He found a force working within him like Paul describes in Romans 7. Evil was now present with him. When he wanted to do good, he found no power to do it. But the evil he did not wish to do he found himself doing. Paul's cry in Romans 7 is "Who shall deliver me from the body of this death?" (Rom. 7:24). It was as though a dead body had been chained to him and he was dragging it around and was killing him. The answer is found in the last verse of Romans 7: "I thank God through Jesus Christ our Lord! So then with the mind I serve the law of God but with the flesh the law of sin" (Rom. 7:25).

Again, I stress this fallen, sinful state did not take Adam's free will and choice and the knowledge of what is morally right. He still had the ability to turn to the Lord rather than hide from Him. Today, the unconverted man or woman has that same right and ability to choose. For someone to forfeit heaven and one day find themselves in hell is not of God's doing or choice but theirs. In Romans 1:19–20, Paul makes it clear that none will have any excuse for there is an inner witness within everyone and that also in creation, His invisible attributes are visible—even His eternal power and Godhead (Rom. 1:20). These verses alone teach us that the responsibility to know God and be born again lies with the sinner. God has given His Son and has not taken away from any of us a free will and the ability to discern the reality of God in creation as well as recognize the God shaped hole and vacuum within every one of our hearts.

From this fallen state and sinful depravity, there is the power of the Gospel that can change, transform, and raise man up and bring him back into a living powerful relationship with God.

As we continue through Romans 8, the one time enemy of the church speaks of a definite and dynamic relationship with God. The Spirit of adoption has entered his heart; he is now in a Father-son relationship with God. The Holy Spirit is a living witness within that not only is he a child of God but also an heir of God and joint heir with Jesus Christ (vv. 15–16).

What Paul is suffering for the Gospel is of no real relevance when compared to the glory that will be revealed in him one day. He is now with all creation waiting, longing, and anticipating the return of Christ—when one day, the whole of creation will be delivered from its bondage and the sons of God will be revealed for the entire world to see.

From a state of spiritual darkness and being a captive to a selfish, fallen nature, from the utter deception and blindness that had once held him in bondage, the Gospel came. It convicted him, changed him, delivered him, and took him from the depths of sinful depravity to the heights of Father-son relationship as a joint heir with Jesus Christ and an heir of the Father. Why would Paul ever feel ashamed of this gospel? It had changed his life; his eternal destiny; and had brought him to know the truth, real purpose, and freedom.

This same power was at work in the Book of the Acts of the Apostles. Three thousand converted on the day of Pentecost and then multitudes in Acts 5. Multitudes responded to the Gospel message as Philip preached in Samaria in Acts 8. A whole household were saved as we read in Acts 10.

To the Corinthian Church, Paul determined that he would preach Christ and Him crucified (1 Cor. 2:2). This message obviously changed lives as Paul reminds them of the fact that some of them were once fornicators, idolaters, adulterers, homosexuals, sodomites, thieves, covetous drunkards, revilers, and extortioners. But they had been washed, sanctified (set apart), and justified (declared just and righteous as if they had never sinned) in the name of the Lord Jesus and by the Holy Spirit (1 Cor. 6:9–11).

The power of the Gospel had turned the city of Ephesus upside down; revival was evident as the people turned from idolatry and the occult and burned all their books on magical arts as a testimony to their newfound faith (Acts 19). The good work that had begun in the believers of Philippi was the transformation of the power of the Gospel (Phil. 1:6). The church at Thessalonica was no exception. Indeed, in just a few short weeks of Paul's visit, the church was planted, and transformation was evident as the people had turned from idols to serve the living and true God and lived in anticipation of the coming of the Lord (1 Thess. 1:9–10).

Down the centuries, the power of the Gospel continued to change people's lives.

Martin Luther is known as the man who ignited the Protestant Reformation. He was born in 1483 into a strict German Catholic family. His parents wanted him to pursue a law career, but he became a monk and a theology professor instead. A sensitive soul, he struggled mightily with a guilty conscience and an intense fear of God and hell. He would confess his sins as many as twenty times per day and lay on a cold concrete floor as penance for his sins until one day he had a revelation of the doctrine of justification by faith while studying the book of Romans. Luther was transformed by the power of the truth of the Gospel, and the Protestant Reformation began.

John Wesley who founded the Methodist movement, along with his brother Charles and George Whitfield, was born in 1703 in Epworth some twenty-three miles from Lincoln, England. John was the fifteenth child of Samuel and Susanna Wesley. His upbringing was very strict and religious. It is said of his mother, who had nineteen children, that she would throw her apron over her head at a certain time of the day and the children knew they had to be quiet as that was the time when their mother was praying.

John's Father was the rector of Epworth 1696. John was only five years old when a fire broke out in the rectory on February 9, 1709. The roof caught fire, and as cries from the streets awakened the Wesleys, they managed to rescue all their children except John who was on the upper floor by himself. Fortunately, before the roof collapsed, John was rescued and lifted out of the upper window. John Wesley referred to the phrase, quoting Zechariah 3:2, as "a brand plucked out of the fire." God had spared his life for what would eventually be a life of destiny that would burn a trail for the Gospel across the world.

It was in later life that John Wesley became a missionary to Georgia. It was after a two-year period that he returned to London feeling beaten down. He attended a meeting in Aldersgate, London, where he listened to the preface of the book of Romans. He noted the time as quarter to nine in the evening. It was as he listened to the description of how Christ can change the human heart that he felt his heart strangely warmed within him. He felt that he did trust in Christ and that he had taken his sins away and was filled with assurance. A short time after this, John Wesley preached on salvation in Christ and the grace of God.

A man changed by the power of the Gospel was now on course to bring the power of the Gospel to multitudes as he journeyed from town to town on horseback.

William Booth was born in 1829. He was converted to Christ by attending a Methodist church in Nottingham, England. Booth was an evangelist and could never settle into a pastorate. The Methodist Church always wanted to push him into pastoral ministry, but William Booth wanted to continue his evangelistic ministry. He thus resigned from the Methodist movement and eventually formed what became known as the Salvation Army.

As Booth saw the poor and homeless on the streets of London, he realized that before the hungry will listen to the Gospel, they needed food in their stomachs. This became the social welfare philosophy and one of the great hallmarks of the Salvation Army. During his lifetime, he established the Salvation Army in fifty-eight countries. This is the power of the Gospel.

In more modern times, we have the countless stories of young men and women who have been delivered from a life of drugs and crime through the Teen Challenge Ministry. My first visit to the USA many years ago was to a church in Los Angeles where around 90 percent of the large congregation were all ex-drug addicts who had been saved and delivered. The pastor of that church had been a mainline heroin addict for thirteen years who had come into contact with the Teen Challenge Ministry in New York. Overnight, he was saved and delivered.

Years before this, a young country preacher was moved as he read in the newspaper of several young men who were to appear in court on a drug-related murder charge. That young country preacher was David Wilkerson. His heart was touched much like Nehemiah's of old when he learned of the devastation of Jerusalem. Nehemiah left Babylon to go and rebuild the walls that had been broken down and the gates that had been burned with fire. David Wilkerson went to seek to rescue lives who had been devastated with drug addiction, where the devil seemed to have free access to their minds and actions—the walls of the knowledge of God had never existed; entrance into their lives by the devil was wide open. The work that was needed was a "rescue work," not a rebuilding. The Teen Challenge Ministry was thus born. That work still goes on in many countries around the world. Countless thousands have been rescued and delivered by the power of the Gospel.

I well remember regularly visiting a prisoner doing a life sentence for murder in a local prison not far from where we lived in the UK. His life had been dramatically transformed by the power of the Gospel. For some forty-five minutes during those visits, he would talk to me of his Bible studies and what he had learned. From being broken with guilt and remorse when first entering prison, he had been visited by the prison chaplain and surrendered his life to Christ. He was changed by the power of the Gospel.

My conversion took place when I was just seventeen years of age. My uncle had married and been persuaded by his wife's brother to attend a local church. This was somewhat unusual as none of us in our immediate family were churchgoers. We were not atheists; we did believe there was a God but had never realized we could actually know Him. His frequent visits to us on weekends were filled with what had been happening at the church he attended. And then it happened. He told us on one of those visits that he had been saved!

I had no idea what he was talking about. My first thoughts were that he had been swimming and nearly drowned. We asked him as many hard questions as we could think of. If he didn't know the answer, he would come back the following weekend and give us an answer after asking his pastor.

Looking back, I think it was his genuine belief and sense of joy and peace that really touched my heart and set me on course to search for the truth. I remember going to a little church about one mile from where we lived and hearing probably for the first time the Gospel of Jesus Christ. Several weeks later in one of those Sunday-evening Gospel meetings, I surrendered my life to Jesus Christ. I prayed much for my parents and grandparents; and over the course of the next twelve months, they all came to know the Lord. We were baptized in water together. What a celebration that was!

My dad was not for coming to church for a while during those first twelve months, although I witnessed many times and pleaded with him to come. I must admit that some of the things I said were quite blunt and not really taken from the textbook of personal witnessing. Eventually, he gave in to my incessant invitations and started to attend. We lived in a little coal-mining village in the heart of Nottinghamshire, England. When I left school at the age of fifteen, as the custom was in those days, I started work as a trainee at the local coal mine which was literally only three hundred yards away from our home. My dad had been attending church for a few months but had never made a commitment to Christ; his conversion came one night through a vivid dream.

He dreamt that he and I had gone to work early one morning. We had stepped into the lift or elevator—better known to the miners as "the cage"—which would slowly take us down to the pit bottom, some several hundred feet underground. The winding gear that lowered the cage started, and the cage began to slowly descend until the cables snapped suddenly and the cage was hurtling to the bottom to what would be certain death.

The miners who were with us, along with my Dad, were scream-ing out with fear when suddenly, the top of the cage flung open and I shot up toward the surface. And as I was disappearing, my dad was shouting my name, "Keith, Keith!" It was at this point that God spoke to him and simply said, "Keith is saved. You are not!" At this moment, he woke up in a cold sweat; and shortly after that, as he walked to work early that morning, he asked Christ to forgive him and to become his Savior. His life changed from that moment.

It has been my joy and greatest privilege over the years to see people wonderfully saved and transformed as I have preached the Gospel, both in local churches and around the world. The Gospel of Jesus Christ still carries the same power today.

This is the Gospel we preach.

13

The Great Exchange

The Gospel offers a great exchange. When people exchange things, most of the time, they have grown tired of the thing to be exchanged and usually are exchanging for something that they consider will be more beneficial. In Scripture, in the prophecy in Isaiah 61, we find what we have called the great exchange. Take note of this passage:

> The Spirit of the Lord God is upon Me, because He has anointed Me to preach good tidings to the poor; He has sent me to heal the brokenhearted, to proclaim liberty to the captives, and the opening of the prison to those who are bound. To proclaim the acceptable year of the Lord, and the day of vengeance of our God; to comfort all who mourn, to console those who mourn in Zion, to give them beauty for ashes, the oil of joy for mourning, the spirit of praise for the spirit of heaviness; that they may be called trees of righteousness, the planting of the Lord, that he may be glorified. (Isa. 61:1–3)

It was this prophecy and portion of scripture that Jesus read from when He stood up in the synagogue in Nazareth after having fasted for forty days. This was an emphatic declaration of who He was and the announcement that sparked hostility from the religious world (Luke 4:28–30). He was taken out of the city, and they were intent on throwing Him off a cliff. For that kind of reaction, it is obvious that what was stated stirred up the forces of darkness. There is always resistance to this kind of message. The devil wants to keep his captives and will do all he can to deceive and keep people from hearing and understanding that the great exchange is on offer.

As Jesus read from the prophecy of Isaiah, He read concerning the "acceptable year of the Lord" (v. 19), which is obviously linked with what the Jews understood regarding the year of Jubilee. Every fiftieth year was to be announced as a year of Jubilee. There are three things that we need to note concerning this: (1) Any Israelite who was in any kind of bondage to any of their own countrymen was to be set free. (2) Ancestral possessions that were sold to aid them in their poverty were to be returned. (3) The Jubilee year was to be a year of rest for the land and the people had to live off what had been produced previously.

The phrase *the acceptable year of the Lord* was a year to celebrate release from burdens and debts and a restoring of possessions. Jesus actually stated, after reading this passage (as his listeners were assembled in the synagogue), that the scripture was fulfilled on that day! He declared that He had come to bring a "spiritual Jubilee" into the hearts of men and women.

The anointing He had received by the Holy Spirit was "to bring good news to the poor" (Isa. 61:1). It is said that the common people were the ones who readily responded to His message, although Jesus made it clear that whoever would come to Him He would never turn away, whether they were rich or poor. The offer is for everyone, whatever social class of society they come from. I'm sure also that the word *poor* means those who are *poor in spirit*. It was when Jesus sat on a mountain one day and began to speak about principles that lead to a blessed life that He said, "Blessed are the poor in spirit for theirs is the kingdom of heaven" (Matt. 5:3). To be "poor in spirit" is to recognize one's sin and failings. Until we do, there can be no repentance; and without repentance, there is no forgiveness and salvation.

Just as in the year of Jubilee there was liberty from slavery, Jesus declared liberty and freedom from the bondage of sin's power and Satan's domination. Spiritual prison doors would be unlocked, and freedom would come bursting in.

As Paul and Silas, imprisoned in Philippi, sang praises to God at the midnight hour, God shook the jail with an earthquake; and the prison door swung open wide (Acts 16). But that wasn't the only door that night that swung open. The jailor who had been listening was convicted of sin (became poor in spirit) and fell down before Paul and Silas, asking what he must do to be saved. Other prison doors also swung open within a short time after that, because the jailor took Paul and Silas home, and before the dawn broke, his whole family were saved and baptized in water. Spiritual Jubilee came to the jailor and his family!

Imagine those first church meetings in the city of Philippi. The jailor and his family would be there along with Lydia and her household and probably the little slave girl who had been possessed by a demon but had received her own personal Jubilee. She would be in attendance, eagerly awaiting the Word of God to be taught, along with others who had heard the message in Philippi.

The vision Paul had received to go to Macedonia (Acts 16) was a call for help, so Paul went with a message of Jubilee. When these new converts assembled together, there must have been a sense of awe and thanksgiving as they looked back on the miracles that had taken place and recognized that their spiritual chains had been broken and that their lives would never be the same. Paul received the vision, and to see the vision become a reality, he had to be obedient.

Immediately, Paul and Silas set sail from Troas (Acts 16:10–12). What they didn't know was the opposition that awaited them. God doesn't always tell us everything about the journey, and maybe that is a good thing. Otherwise, we may not want to take it. However, we can be sure of one thing: if God has called us to go, He will be with us on the journey, whatever happens. He is still the God who causes all things to work together for our good. Even the imprisonment turned out to be Jubilee for the jailor and his family.

There was no Facebook for Paul on which to post pictures of the newly formed church, and he didn't take a glossy picture album of his missionary endeavors back with him. He only had the scars on his back from the thirty-nine stripes he had received before being thrown into prison. However, to Paul, his reward was to leave a church behind of men and women and their families rejoicing in Jubilee.

"This is the acceptable year of the Lord," said Jesus, referencing Isaiah 61:2. Isaiah prophesied before that Israel the ten northern tribes were taken into captivity by Assyria and also warned Judah of impending judgment. His message is one of warning and preparation as well as hope for the future, although the exile to Babylon did not take place until about one hundred years after Isaiah's death. Isaiah did not know the timing of this and began to prepare the people.

When we come to the second half of this book and Isaiah 61, which we are considering, this is a direct prophecy of the coming Messiah and the future hope, restoration, and blessing of Israel. The apostle Paul writes of the restoration of Israel in Romans 11:1: "I say then, has God cast away His people? Certainly not! For I am an Israelite, of the seed of Abraham, of the tribe of Benjamin." The whole chapter speaks of the Gentile nations being brought into salvation because of Israel's blindness and rejection of the Messiah, but then goes onto write of the great blessing that will come as Israel turns to the Lord (Rom. 11:12–15).

Isaiah 61 is a direct reference to the coming of the Messiah (Jesus), regarding His ministry on earth and also further references to His second coming. We are now living in "the acceptable year of the Lord," and the great exchange is now on offer.

To understand this, we must go back to Isaiah 53. Isaiah prophesies of the rejection of Christ: "He is despised and rejected by men, a man of sorrows and acquainted with grief. And we hid our faces from Him; He was despised, and we did not esteem Him" (Isa. 53:3).

The prophet then shows us the basis on which God offers the great exchange. Take note of the following passages:

- Isaiah 53:5—"He was wounded for our transgressions. He was bruised for our iniquities: the chastisement for our peace was upon Him, and by His stripes we are healed."
- Isaiah 53:6—"All we like sheep have gone astray: we have turned every one to his own way, and the Lord has laid on Him the iniquity of us all."
- Isaiah 53:8—"For the transgression of my people He was stricken."
- Isaiah 53:12—"And He was numbered with the transgressors, and He bore the sin of many, and made intercession for the transgressors."

The only way that God could offer such a great exchange, as recorded in Isaiah 61, is because Christ took our sins and judgment upon the cross. And God was willing and even "pleased to bruise Him: and put Him to grief" (v. 10). The only reason God was "pleased" to allow His Son to be led like a lamb to the slaughter was that He might bless us with His salvation. He took our sins so that we would not have to take the judgment. He was bruised so that we might be blessed. He was wounded and afflicted that we might enter into the great exchange.

It is interesting to note that Luke does not record Jesus reading any further than the line, which states, "He had come to proclaim the acceptable year of the Lord." He did not read the next line, which says, "And the day of vengeance of our God."

It is true to say that when Christ died upon the cross, He did bring judgment upon our greatest enemy—that is, the devil (Heb. 2:14). Although, as previously stated, Satan is still allowed to roam free, he has not been cast into the lake of fire yet. However, he is limited to what he can do and knows the day of real vengeance is yet to come. At Christ's second coming, Paul reveals that He will come with flames of fire "taking vengeance on them that do not obey the Gospel of Jesus Christ" (2 Thess. 1:8–9). Jesus chose not to read this; but to leave his listeners with the thought that "the acceptable year of the Lord" was now on hand.

With the "acceptable year of the Lord," comfort is on offer. When comfort is offered, it is for those who are grieving over some loss or hardship, for those who have been ravaged by the storms of life whose hopes have been shattered and dreams lost. Sin has left its mark and scars with everyone; some have been left on the scrap heap of guilt and shame. Their memories are a constant reminder of what might have been; and grief has become their companion, robbing them of sleep, peace, and hope. But this doesn't have to continue. Things can change just as they did in the year of Jubilee. Freedom and comfort is on offer for this is the "acceptable year of the Lord."

As Jesus read through the verses of Isaiah 61, He outlined the exchange that was on offer by saying there was not only comfort but "beauty for ashes." Ashes in the Bible were used as a sign and admission of guilt or an expression of sorrow for sins and also as a pledge to reform and resist temptation. When Jonah preached repentance in Nineveh—although very reluctantly—his message had this profound effect: repentance hit the city.

Jonah warned Nineveh would be overthrown in forty days. The people believed God had proclaimed a fast and put on sackcloth and ashes. Even the king covered himself with sackcloth and ashes and proclaimed a fast and published it throughout Nineveh. Judgment was turned away by the Lord who saw their works. The prophet Daniel put on sackcloth and ashes on behalf of his people for their rebellion and wickedness (Dan. 9:3).

Ashes are the remains, the dust, of something that once was. You can look at a heap of ashes and there is no chance of restoration or recovery to become what those ashes once were. Ashes speak of finality, despair, and hopelessness. When we apply that thought to our lives, there are so many things that can happen that can seemingly leave us staring at a heap of ashes. Some people never recover from the storms of life; so ravaged by them that despair and depression heap upon them ashes for the rest of their days.

We live in a world that is full of amazing technology but offers no hope of lifting someone from the ashes of grief and tragedy. If we are totally unprepared, the shock and the unbelief that hits during the loss of a loved one leaves so many of us in ashes. The future is bleak and the memories hurt and the remedy seems non-existent. We see it portrayed every day across the world on our TV screens—families are left with ashes as tornados sweep away what they have lived and saved for all their lives; war and terrorism are too close when they happen within our own streets and cities and always leaving behind ashes in its wake, and lives left devastated with the thought *How could any other human being do such a thing?* in our minds.

Once-happy families are left in ruins through divorce on the grounds of unfaithfulness, greed, lust, and selfishness; and a spouse is left with just a heap of ashes—wondering if anyone can ever be trusted again, feeling rejection and grief, not because they have lost someone but the love of their life walking out on them. Marriage vows are cast aside and so have their future lives together.

When I refer to *ashes*, I am talking about the pain, the hurt, the scars, and the grief that people are left with—a business deal gone wrong, the economy taking a nose dive, mortgages too high, and wages that are no longer because of job loss. I am talking about the looming foreclosure, the bills mounting up, the increasing worries, and the stress levels at breaking point. The human heart cries out for an answer but sees only ashes of what once it enjoyed.

These are the broken promises, the dreams that never materialized, and the prayers that seemed to go unanswered. Questions of *Why me, Lord, why did this happen?* loom over us in these times. These are the times when you may have thought like Mary and Martha when their brother Lazarus died—"If only the Lord had shown up, it could have all been avoided"—the mistakes that have been made, the wrong decisions, the sins that haunt and torment.

Ashes are everywhere. You see them with the homeless begging on the street corner. You see them with the rich and famous; behind the smiles of their so-called success there is so often an emptiness that is still searching for truth. You see them in the rehabilitation programs as people struggle with addictions. You see them behind bars in the correctional centers across the land. You see them in the worried looks and bloodshot eyes of men and women who have been dealt ashes.

There are so many scenarios that could be mentioned. Even the disciples saw only ashes of what once was for three days between the crucifixion and resurrection. But then it all changed. The One who had walked on water and calmed the storm was alive. Death had not beaten Him; He had beaten death. And with His resurrection, a new day dawned for His followers. He stepped into the room where they were assembled and, with one smile, scattered the ashes of grief and despair from their lives. If you feel like you have been left with ashes, then here is the good news: There is a crown of beauty instead of ashes. This is the great exchange.

Notice the phrase *a crown of beauty* instead of ashes. There is nothing beautiful about despair, depression, and hopelessness; those are the things that destroy natural beauty. Jesus was offering a "crown of beauty." Crowns speak of authority. It is the picture of a new position. Instead of ashes covering the head, it's a crown of authority. Instead of being the victim to despair, it's becoming the victor. The victors wear the crown, not victims!

There are some things that every one of us remembers from childhood as though it was just yesterday, and they seem to be indelibly etched in our minds. For me, one of these is the day when my dad had planted some lettuce seeds in the garden when I was probably about seven or eight years of age. The lettuce had broken through the soil and seemed to be doing well until we had several days of hot weather and no rain.

I remember one of these young lettuce plants bowed over, dying from lack of water. My dad filled his watering can and poured some on this little lettuce; and there before my eyes, it immediately straightened up and looked refreshed. It was completely revived! It was like it had just exchanged ashes for a crown of beauty! That is the picture here that Isaiah was painting.

Our history is not our destiny. Our past does not have to dictate our future. Yesterday's failings do not have to ruin our tomorrows. Adam lost authority when he sinned, but Jesus died not only to be our substitute and Savior but to restore authority back to those who are prepared to step from under the ashes and kneel at the foot of the cross. It is there He crowns the sinner with salvation; authority; and the beauty of His presence, peace, and grace.

Not only is there beauty for ashes, but He also promises the "oil of joy for mourning" (Isa. 61:3). Mourning, sorrow, and remorse can all be exchanged for the "oil of joy." It was said that Jesus was anointed with the oil of gladness above His companions because He loved righteousness and hated iniquity (Heb. 1:9). Despite knowing all that He had come to do by way of crucifixion, Jesus was filled with joy. The Kingdom of God that Jesus came to bring into the hearts of men and women is characterized by "righteousness, peace and joy in the Holy Spirit" (Rom. 14:17).

The oil or ointment was used at times of great gladness; this is the kind of oil Jesus was promising to pour into the hearts of those who mourn over sin. Joy is a wonderful theme of the Bible. Real joy only comes with assurance of salvation and with the confidence we have in the Word of God that our sin has been judged and paid for by the death of Christ.

Too often, we have had the picture painted in our minds of a Christ who was "the man of sorrows" and who somehow was not really human—that He was a man who stood out in the crowd with His long, flowing hair and beautiful eyes. In fact, he was quite ordinary looking. Even Judas, when betraying Him, had to make Him known to the soldiers who had come to arrest Him by kissing Him on the cheek. The prophet Isaiah wrote that "when we see Him there is no beauty that we should desire Him" (Isa. 53:2).

Picture someone bowed low with the heavy weight of sin, guilt, and despair; and suddenly, this is exchanged for great joy—the kind of joy that comes when a sinner realizes that the load and weight of sin has been carried by someone else, when the invisible prison bars of guilt are removed, and the door that had been locked to bar the prisoner from true liberty now open. When the prisoner walks through the door, joy springs up in his heart, freedom beckons, and the joy of knowing that freedom sweeps away the grief and mourning.

When Peter and John commanded the lame man (who had been laid at the gate of the Temple day after day for many years) to rise, he started walking leaping and praising God (Acts 3). One moment, he had been begging, and it was just another mundane day; the next moment, it was like someone had swept away his ashes and poured upon him the oil of joy. It was no good trying to ask this man to be quiet; he had just experienced a miracle—no more ashes, no more mourning. He had been set free, healed, in the name of Jesus.

When Peter wrote his first letter—specifically, in 1 Peter 1:8—he wrote of a joy that is unspeakable or inexpressible. Although these believers had not seen Christ, they had come to know Him. The kind of joy the Bible speaks of is not dependent on circumstances or if everything seems to be going our way; it is much deeper than that. Peter wrote to people who were going through trials and hardships, and yet they had great joy (1 Pet. 1:6). This kind of joy comes through knowing and understanding the great message of the Gospel. Peter writes of God's abundant mercy and a living hope through the resurrection of Christ from the dead. Also an inheritance—which is incorruptible, undefiled, and does not fade away—this is reserved in heaven for all believers. He also assures them that, in this journey through life despite all the trials, they are to be kept by the power of God through faith, for all that He has in store for them in this amazing salvation (1 Pet. 1:3–5).

They had their eyes on eternity!

The apostle Paul could say, despite prophetic warnings of his arrest, if he journeyed to Jerusalem, none of those things would move

Him from the will of God, in order that he may finish his race with joy and the ministry of the grace of God (Acts 20:22–24). When we read through the New Testament, there are so many instances where believers were going through difficult times, even Paul knew shipwrecks and beatings. They went through great persecution and trials but maintained this amazing joy. Much of modern preaching sugarcoats the Gospel; we hear so much about the favor of God that sometimes it leaves people with the thought that, if they are going through tough times, God has deserted them. That is never the case, and that is not what the Bible teaches. As my wife and I have traveled to third-world countries, we have seen hardships and poverty among many of the believers; but despite their lack of material things, there is so often a sense of great gratitude to God and a deep-seated joy that comes from a living relationship with the Lord.

The great exchange is on offer. Jesus also offers the "garment of praise for the spirit of heaviness" (Isa. 61:3). The sackcloth and ashes of sin and guilt are removed, and the beauty of His presence is restored. Instead of a spirit of heaviness, there is a spirit of praise. There is something liberating about praise. God loves to manifest His presence through praise. It is faith released along with thankfulness and gratitude to the grace of God. Praise takes our eyes off our own problems and centers them on the goodness and faithfulness of God. The Psalms are full of exhortations to praise the Lord; in fact, if we have breath we are exhorted to praise the Lord (Ps. 150:6).

Keep this passage in mind: "Praise the Lord! For it is good to sing praises to our God; for it is pleasant and praise is beautiful ... He heals the broken hearted and binds up their wounds" (Ps. 147:1, 3).

The psalmist encouraged instruments such as the trumpet, lute, and harp; the flutes and loud clashing symbols were used. It gives the impression that praise is demonstrative; and while it can take on many forms, God is not afraid of noise and dance.

I remember being in Jerusalem many years ago; and just as the Sabbath was commencing, a group of young Israeli students was making their way toward the Wailing Wall. They danced together as they held hands. To dance was part of their culture and had been from the times of the Old Testament. It was said of David that "he danced with all his might". When David was bringing back the ark of the Lord to Jerusalem, it was a time of celebration, thanksgiving and praise, (2 Sam. 6:14).

The ark represented the presence of God, and David wanted to bring back God's presence to Jerusalem, knowing that the worship and praise of the Lord must be central to the life of the nation. They brought the ark of the Lord to Jerusalem with shouting and the sound of trumpets (2 Sam. 6:15). When David danced, he actually was leaping and whirling before the Lord (2 Sam. 6:16). He had prepared a tent in Jerusalem to place the ark in; and as he and the celebrating procession came into the city, David was not ashamed to show his exuberance in his dancing. It is interesting that his wife, Michal, criticized him for his public display, which she had seen from her window when he came dancing back into the city (2 Sam. 6:20–23). She cast scorn upon him for "uncovering" himself, which simply means he had taken off his royal robe and was like the rest.

David's answer was direct and decisive: "I will be more undignified than this and will be humble in my own sight" (2 Sam. 6:22). The interesting thing is that verse 23 says, "Therefore Michal the daughter of Saul had no children to the day of her death." She remained barren! Maybe she couldn't take the praise and public displays of celebration to the Lord because her father, Saul, had neglected the worship of the Lord and she was a woman who had idols in her house (1 Sam. 9:13). Her heart was not right, so she despised her husband and she remained barren.

God's will is never for us to remain spiritually barren, but true praise and worship cannot be offered from a heart filled with idolatry and resentment. When the church meets together, we should enjoy great times of corporate worship and praise, centering our hearts on the One who has done so much for us. Don't allow your own reservations to hold you back from praise and break through the barrier!

After all, what God calls us into is not a religious order but a dynamic love relationship with Himself.

David, the psalmist, spoke to his soul, "Why are you cast down O my soul and why are you disquieted within me?" (Ps. 42). (I often remark it is OK to speak to yourself, the problem comes when we start answering ourselves back!) David commences this Psalm by a longing and thirsting to meet with God. He describes it like the hart that would pant after water brooks, leaping from one crag to another in search of water. David was looking back to the times when he would join the worshippers in the house of God but now was in a situation where that was not possible (Ps. 42:4). Despite all circumstances, the psalmist spoke to his soul and declared that he would hope in God and would yet praise Him. We are encouraged to praise the Lord and not to forget all His benefits (Ps. 103).

He forgives all our iniquities, heals all our diseases, redeems our lives from destruction and crowns us with loving kindness and tender mercies, and fills our mouth or life with good things. We should never forget all that God has done for us but constantly keep our hearts in a state of thankfulness and praise. We are dealing not just with the benefits we may experience in this life but with eternal blessings. There is something very refreshing being in the presence of someone whose life is filled with praise.

Sometimes, we may feel like the psalmist, cast down through circumstances; but the apostle Peter encourages us to bring forth a sacrifice of praise. Sacrifice costs us something, and to bring praise to the Lord when everything within us feels cast down demands we rise above feelings and hope in God. Faith kicks in, and we dig down into our spirit in order to bring forth the kind of praise that God looks for and loves.

Over the years, we have been amazed at the people we have met and those whom we have had the privilege of being their pastor. Each had their own story of the faithfulness and grace of God that kept them in sometimes dire circumstances. These may be people who have gone through the valley of grief as their child or children have died. Others may have suffered the loss of a spouse. Some may have had their businesses failed and houses went to foreclosure, while others have battled cancer and life-threatening illnesses. There could be so many other scenarios that could be mentioned, but to look over a congregation on Sunday morning and see these same people praising the Lord is a testimony to the grace of God. I have to believe that God looks down and is well pleased with His masterpiece; but I think that more than looking down on us, He steps into the midst of a praising people and takes delight as they praise Him for who He is. That kind of praise must send the principalities and powers into total confusion and disarray!

The psalmist David wrote Psalm 22:3, which says, "But You are holy, enthroned in the praises of Israel." The word *enthroned* is also translated "inhabits." This brings us the picture of God actually being right in the midst of our praise as the King who sits upon His throne. I am sure every believer would long for the King of kings to come and manifest His presence in the midst of the congregation. This psalm reveals how that can actually take place. It happens when the church rises to bring praise and worship to the One who has redeemed us. Imagine the kind of effect that would have upon everyone gathered!

We are sometimes so concerned with unbelievers not being put off by any exuberant praise that we often miss the opportunity of the real presence of God. I am not suggesting that all praise have to be of a demonstrative nature—God sees the hearts of people—and wherever there is true praise, He is in the midst, inhabiting the praise. It is my firm belief, if we believers would bring real praise from hearts that are overcome with God's goodness, we would see manifestations of His glory. Imagine then the effect that would have not only upon the church but upon unbelievers who were present!

Cold, formal religion is not what the world longs for; the world is and will be as the time draws near for Christ to return—that is, looking for the reality of God. A God who can meet them at their point of need, a God who can gather up the ashes of lives that have been devastated by sin and give them hope and new life, is the God we long for. The Holy Spirit can do more in moments like that than we can do in a lifetime. When people come in to contact and experience God for themselves, lives change, deep-seated problems and strongholds (thought patterns) are broken, inner hurts are healed, forgiveness flows, and bitterness flees. There is power in praise and worship.

The God who gives us the great exchange wants us to enjoy His presence. He is our Father, and we are His children. He loves us, wants the best for us, loves to be in our midst, and manifests Himself to us. We have to learn that singing a few songs is not always the summit of our praise and worship; there has to be a longing and desire on our part to break through and sometimes break out of our self-imposed boundaries and press through into His glory with praise and worship. We are called to offer up spiritual sacrifices acceptable to God through Jesus Christ (1 Pet. 2:5). Praise is one of those sacrifices, but always remember that it is the Lord who has given us a spirit of praise in exchange for heaviness. The least we can do is to offer that back to Him, who is worthy to be praised.

To return to the story of David and the bringing back of the ark to Jerusalem, where he had prepared a tent, what he did is so often missed and misunderstood. The tabernacle of David, or the tent he had prepared, was so different from the tabernacle of Moses. David appointed singers and singing (1 Chron. 15:16–27; 25:1–7). No singers sang in the tabernacle of Moses. Musicians were also appointed to play and sing before the Lord (1 Chron. 23:5; 25:1–7). David also delivered a psalm into the hand of Asaph and his brethren to thank the Lord; in it, they were encouraged to "glory in His holy name and to let the hearts of those who seek the Lord, rejoice" (1 Chron. 16:8–10).

The atmosphere in David's tabernacle was so vastly different from that of the tabernacle of Moses. Other heathen religions had no joy, no celebrations with rejoicing; but in David's tabernacle, this was the order. We have the mystery that was kept secret from the foundation of the world—"Christ in us the hope of Glory" (Col. 1:27—we have everything to rejoice in and to praise the Lord for. What a great exchange! It's time to put on the garment of praise and take off the spirit of heaviness.

You may have garments hung in your closet that you have never worn. The choice is yours as to whether you wear them or not. God has given us the spirit of praise. It's time for every believer to enter into the exchange. The enemy will resist you because the manifestation of God's presence is waiting to descend upon you as an individual and upon the corporate gatherings of God's people. Thank God for the great exchange may we live it out.

I am reminded of the words of an old Gospel song, "Something Beautiful" by the Gaither Vocal Band, that says,

> If ever there were dreams that were lofty and noble, they were my dreams from the start, and the hopes for life's best were the hopes that I harbored down deep in my heart, but my castles all crumbled, my dreams turned to ashes, my fortunes turned to loss, so I wrapped them all in the rags of my life, and laid then at the cross, "Something beautiful, something good, all my confusion He understood, all I had to offer Him was brokenness and strife, but He made something beautiful out of my life."

The great exchange is the Gospel we preach.

14

The Gospel of Signs and Wonders

Jesus gave specific instructions and commands to His disciples that they were to go into all the world and preach the Gospel to every creature. As people believed, they were to be baptized. He also gave the promise that signs would follow those who believe. They were to cast out demons in His name; they would speak with new tongues; take up serpents; and if they were to drink any deadly thing, it would not hurt them. They were also to lay hands on the sick and they would recover (Mark 16:15–18).

Before we consider any of the abovementioned, it seems pretty obvious that the preaching of the Gospel is to be accompanied with appropriate following signs. To read through the Gospels, one has to conclude that Jesus's ministry was accompanied with signs and wonders, as were the early disciples and apostles after Jesus ascended to heaven. The book of the Acts of the Apostles is also filled with many accounts of signs and wonders. Jerusalem was stirred, cities witnessed revival, thousands were saved and healed, and churches planted because of the impact of the Gospel preached with signs and wonders.

In many churches, the truth of signs and wonders has been lost, many believing that these were for the early church and not really for today. If the Gospel is preached, we praise God because it is still the power of God unto salvation. But the signs Jesus spoke of were belonging for the apostolic times and not for today, say many modern preachers. It is my belief that despite the fact that even some charismatic and Pentecostal churches have played down the "signs and wonders" and have been influenced by other methods to bring seekers to Christ, there is a growing renewal and desire to see the supernatural signs and wonders of which the Bible speaks.

I also believe that in the last days, as the Bible speaks about the outpouring of the Holy Spirit, these signs and wonders will come in an even greater measure as the church sees the problems that the world has created are actually fields that are white unto harvest. God will keep the best for the last as He stirs the hearts of His people to again dare to believe for greater works.

Everything the Lord does, the devil seeks to copy and counterfeit. It is interesting following this thought through that when we turn to the book of the Revelation, the Antichrist who is to come will come with signs and lying wonders. If signs and wonders are not important, then why would the enemy of our souls reveal the Antichrist with signs and wonders? The answer to that is simple. Because signs and wonders are convincing.

Now we must understand that everything must be judged by the Word of God and not by supernatural signs; and as I have just stated, the devil is capable of reproducing those. We should not be taken in by someone who simply works signs and wonders, but rather the character of the person must be checked and the truth of the Word of God must always be paramount. Here, I am not dealing with counterfeit signs and wonders but, rather, the kind we see manifested in the Bible as Jesus's disciples obeyed the command to go into all the world.

When Jesus came to earth, though He was—and is—the Son of God, He was also the son of man. He was a human, being born the same way every other human being is born except the conception by Mary was by the Holy Spirit and Joseph was not His father but, rather, His guardian. Nevertheless, every miracle He performed was by the Holy Spirit and not by virtue of being the Son of God. Jesus could turn to His disciples and say "Greater works than these shall you do because I go to the Father" (John 14:12).

The key phrase to consider is *because I go to the Father*. Jesus was promising them that when He returned to the Father, He would send the Holy Spirit. Jesus referred to the Holy Spirit as "another helper" (John 14:16, 26; 15:26; 16:7). The Holy Spirit was to be sent to be alongside the disciples and also to be within them. Jesus declared, "If any man thirsts that he should come to Him and drink and he who believes would experience flowing from his innermost being rivers of living water" (John 7:37–38).

The Holy Spirit of which He spoke had not yet been given at that time. Rather, the Father had a specific time already chosen for the giving or outpouring of the Holy Spirit. It was to be the day of Pentecost when thousands would gather in Jerusalem for the Feast of Pentecost. The feast was a yearly celebration of the first fruits of the harvest. Jesus would then be back in heaven, having been crucified, risen, and ascended.

Over the years, there has been much debate regarding the Holy Spirit, especially the doctrine called the "baptism of the Holy Spirit." It has been confused by many with what the Bible calls the "baptism into the body of Christ."

In 1 Corinthians 12, Paul is teaching regarding the various gifts that the Holy Spirit gives to believers and stressing the fact that all believers are members of one body—Christ—and whatever gift or gifts we have been given are all needed for the effective functioning of the body of Christ, which is the church. The question we must ask is, At what point is a person baptized into the body of Christ? Obviously, from the chapter, we are considering it is the Holy Spirit who brings a believer into (or baptizes into) the body of Christ.

In previous chapters, I have written of the miracle of the new birth, which cannot take place without the work of the Holy Spirit. Jesus made that clear to Nicodemus (John 3) when He spoke of being born again of the Holy Spirit. We have also Paul in Romans 8 teaching that the Holy Spirit bears witness with our spirit and the result is assurance and the knowledge that God is our Father. The cry from our heart is "Abba Father" (Rom. 8:15). Every believer has the Holy Spirit indwelling them; that is very clear from such scriptures. The problem for many is, trying to explain the happenings of the day of Pentecost and further accounts of the outpouring of the Holy Spirit and the supernatural utterances of speaking with tongues, as recorded in the book of the Acts of the Apostles.

Before Jesus ascended to the Father, He breathed upon His disciples and said, "Receive the Holy Spirit, if you forgive the sins of any, they are forgiven them; if you retain the sins of any, they are retained" (John 20:23). What is so often said regarding the outpouring of the Holy Spirit on the day of Pentecost as recorded in (Acts 2). Is that this is when the early disciples were born again and baptized into the Body of Christ. If that is the case, then what happened when Jesus breathed upon them?

To follow the thought through of Jesus breathing upon them, the very first time we see this in scripture is when God breathed into Adam, thus becoming a living soul. The breath of God brought life. Similarly, in Ezekiel 37:4–14, it was God's breath that entered into the dead bodies that lay in the valley of dry bones. It was this same breath that caused them to live.

Paul writes to Timothy and reminds him that "all scripture is given by inspiration of God [or God breathed]" (2 Tim. 3:16)—the Word of God brings life!

When Jesus breathed upon those early disciples, I believe He was breathing life into them through the Holy Spirit; and at that point, they were born again. If they had received the Holy Spirit as in the new birth before Pentecost, we then have a subsequent experience after conversion, which is at Pentecost! In Ephesians 4, Paul lists a number of fundamental truths—seven in all—and included in that list is "one baptism." It may be argued that there cannot be *another* baptism in the Holy Spirit if there is one baptism into the body of Christ. There is also, of course, "water baptism." So Paul, when he lists the seven ones in Ephesians 4:4–6, is urging the church to unity, reminding them that believers are united and related in their faith and that they are to endeavor to keep that unity and not allow anything to divide. The one baptism then is referring to being born again by the Holy Spirit and being placed into the Body of Christ.

If the followers of Jesus who assembled in that upper room in Jerusalem, waiting for the endowment of power by the Holy Spirit, had already received the life of God by the breath of Jesus and had been born again, then what happened at Pentecost was something not only subsequent to salvation but distinct from it. One was the receiving of life and the other the receiving of power. One was to give them new birth and the other was to give them power to take the message of the Gospel to the world.

The other disagreement among evangelicals who believe in the infilling of the Holy Spirit, or the "baptism of the Holy Spirit," is whether *tongues* are the initial evidence of this experience. It would be true to say that there are a number of instances in the book of the Acts of the Apostles that refer to people speaking in tongues as they received the baptism of the Holy Spirit, and there are also a number where tongues are not mentioned. Of course, the fact that *tongues* are not mentioned on some of the occasions does not necessarily mean that this did not happen.

John the Baptist first mentioned this term when referring to the Messiah Jesus, who was to come, while John was baptizing believers in water. He spoke of one who was to come who would "baptize in the Holy Spirit" (Luke 3:16). Water baptism by John was immersion, and the baptism he referred to that Jesus by the Holy Spirit would be an immersion in the Holy Spirit's power.

There can be no doubt that what happened on the day of Pentecost completely transformed those early disciples, including the mother of Jesus who was present. Peter—who had previously denied Christ at the crucial hour of testing and had probably felt the biggest failure of them all after the crucifixion and before the resurrection—was now standing up and delivering a powerful Gospel message. Three thousand repented and were baptized! Peter was changed by God's power; he was bold, he had come out of the shadows of guilt and failure, and he stood up with the message of the Gospel burning in his heart.

The Bible tells us that by the mouth of two or three witnesses, every Word shall be established (2 Cor. 13:1). The book of the Acts of the Apostles has many witnesses to the initial evidence of speaking in tongues when people were baptized with the Holy Spirit.

On the day of Pentecost, as already mentioned, there were one hundred and twenty. Philip went down to Samaria and preached Christ to them (Acts 8:5). Multitudes saw the miracles and believed and were baptized in water (Acts 8:12). There was a man called Simon—who had previously practiced sorcery—who also believed and was baptized. Peter and John had come down from Jerusalem to pray for the new believers that they may receive the Holy Spirit. In Acts 8:16. we have these words regarding the Holy Spirit: "For as yet He had fallen upon none of them. They had only been baptized in the name of the Lord Jesus."

When Simon saw what happened, as Peter and John prayed over these new believers, he offered them money so that he might have this same power—that is, whoever he laid hands upon may also receive the Holy Spirit. The Bible does not state that they spoke in tongues on this occasion, but the question we must ask is obvious, What was it then that Simon saw that convinced him so much, that he was willing to pay money for it? There must have been some evidence, but the scripture is quiet on this occasion; it doesn't say they spoke in tongues, but again, it doesn't say they didn't. However, we cannot appeal to this account in order to prove the initial evidence of speaking with other tongues when someone is baptized with the Holy Spirit.

In Acts 9, we have the account of Saul's conversion. It was Ananias to whom God spoke and told him to go and pray for Saul (Paul) that he would receive his sight. Saul had been blind since his Damascus road experience. Ananias found Saul in the house exactly where the Lord had told him. He found Saul praying and said, "Brother Saul, the Lord Jesus who appeared to you on the road as you came, has sent me that you may receive your sight and be filled with the Holy Spirit" (Acts 9:17).

Scales fell from Saul's eyes, he received his sight, and he was baptized in water. Again, we are not told that he spoke in tongues, but it seems obvious that Saul was converted on the Damascus road when the Lord spoke to him. And yet, the Lord still wanted him to receive the Holy Spirit, which is a subsequent experience to salvation.

We find another amazing story of God directing people and bringing divine connections for His purposes to be fulfilled. Peter is praying on the housetop (Acts 10). The Lord had spoken to a centurion called Cornelius, and He told Cornelius to send some of his servants to the very house where Peter was lodging. Always remember, God sees everything and knows exactly where we are, always listens to our prayers, and has bigger plans than we do!

Peter was to go and speak to the household of Cornelius. How many were in that house waiting for Peter, we do not know; but there could well have been perhaps twenty to thirty, with servants, family, and close friends included. As Peter and some believers from Joppa who accompanied him arrived at the house of Cornelius, they heard Cornelius relate how God had spoken to him.

As Peter began to preach, something happened that had not happened before and was one of those Divine surprises that God throws in now and again. Peter's sermon is interrupted as the Holy Spirit fell upon all those who heard the Word. He had just reached the point of explaining there was remission of sins to those who believe in Christ (Acts 10:44–45). The scripture actually says, "They heard them speak with tongues and magnify God" (Acts 10:46).

Although they were Gentiles, they realized they could not hold them back from being baptized in water. Now, we have possibly at least another twenty witnesses who spoke in tongues when they were baptized with the Holy Spirit. In relating this story to the believers at Jerusalem later, Peter said,

"And as I began to speak the Holy Spirit fell upon them as on us at the beginning. Then I remembered the word of the Lord, how He said: "John indeed baptized with water, but you shall be baptized with the Holy Spirit." (Acts 11:15–16)

Upon arriving in Ephesus, Paul found around twelve disciples and asked them if they had received the Holy Spirit when they had believed. Of course, some argued that that was simply referring to the new birth and the Holy Spirit entering the spirit of the new believer. We need to keep in mind that in the early church, when the Gospel was preached, water baptism and the baptism in the Holy Spirit were part of the whole message of the Good News. They expected people to be baptized almost immediately and to be filled with the Holy Spirit. They believed that these things were foundational and necessary for every believer.

In the account in Acts 19 just mentioned, we have another twelve disciples who spoke with tongues and also prophesied as hands were laid upon them to receive the baptism in the Holy Spirit. One hundred and twenty at Pentecost, another twenty at least at the house of Cornelius, and another twelve in Ephesus adds up to around one hundred and fifty witnesses! And by the way, remember Paul said to the Corinthian Church that he spoke in tongues more than them all (1 Cor. 14:18).

In conversations I have had with individuals over the years, some have not agreed with the initial evidence of speaking with other tongues at the baptism in the Holy Spirit. They believed they were filled with the Holy Spirit without any such evidence. I have chosen not to argue but simply to say to them, if they believe they have received the Holy Spirit, why not ask God for the gift of tongues as the Bible says that this is a gift of God and brings with it a supernatural prayer language? When writing to the Corinthian Church, Paul wished that they all spoke with tongues as this is one of the ways that believers can edify or build themselves up in faith (1 Cor. 14:4–5).

To denigrate these gifts and experiences along with signs and wonders to an apostolic age is to do disservice to the Great Commission Jesus gave to His disciples. Who decided when the apostolic age concluded? Was it when the last apostle died? Was heaven waiting for the final breath of that apostle and then closed the door on the gifts of the Holy Spirit? Who is to say that there are no longer apostles?

Paul teaches us in Ephesians 4:11–16 that apostles, prophets, evangelists, pastors, and teachers are given by the risen Christ for

> the perfecting or equipping of the saints [believers] for the work of the ministry, for the edifying of the body of Christ until we all come to the unity of the faith and of the knowledge of the Son of God to a perfect man to the stature of the fullness of Christ.

If we still need pastors, evangelists, and teachers, then why would we not need apostles and prophets? To imagine that the body of Christ has arrived at the "fullness of the stature of Christ" defies logic; even the churches that Paul planted were not free from carnal problems and doctrinal deviancies. The ministry of the apostle and prophet is still needed today along with all the other ministry gifts.

Some may argue that 1 Corinthians 13 shows us a better way, the way of love. This chapter has been used to prove that love now overrides gifts of the Holy Spirit, and they cite the last verse in the chapter, which says, "And now abide faith hope, love, these three but the greatest of these is love." When Paul wrote this letter, he did not write it in chapters; translators arranged the chapters years later. So 1 Corinthians 14 follows on without a break and should read "The greatest of these is love. Pursue love, and desire spiritual gifts, but especially that you may prophesy" (1 Cor. 14:1).

There is no way that Paul would teach that love has now over-ridden gifts. He spoke in tongues, worked miracles, and saw signs and wonders. The love chapter fits well in between 1 Corinthians 12 and 14 as a reminder that all gifts of the Holy Spirit must be used with the motive of love and not for self-glorification.

> But when that which is perfect is come, then that which is in part will be done away. When I was a child I spoke as a child, I understood as a child, I thought as a child; but when I became a man, I put away childish things. For now we see through a glass dimly, but then face to face. Now I know in part, but then I shall know just as I also am known (1 Corinthians 13:10).

The phrase *when that which is perfect is come* is interpreted by some to mean the scriptures concluding that there is now no need for spiritual gifts. If Paul is referring to Christ's second coming allow me also to take you to what is said in 1 Corinthians 1:7: "So that you come short in no gift, eagerly waiting for the revelation of our Lord Jesus Christ." Paul taught us that the gifts of the Holy Spirit are to be sought and used until Jesus returns in this passage.

I know there have been excesses over the years; but wherever there is excessive blessing, there will be some excesses. The reason Paul wrote to the Corinthians was to help them to be orderly in their use of tongues, interpretation of tongues, and prophesy, among other things. The old saying "Don't throw the baby out with the bath water" holds true. Sometimes, people have been turned off from the gifts of the Holy Spirit because of some bad experience or some excess or showmanship. It's like the person who often says "I can't believe in God because there are too many hypocrites." There are a number of them who attend church every week and live like the world from Monday to Saturday. They do damage to the Christian testimony and are hypocrites (playactors); but always remember, if there is the false, there is also the genuine!

Down the centuries, there have been supernatural encounters with the Holy Spirit. D. L. Moody described his experience, "I kept on crying all the time that God would fill me with His Holy Spirit."

One day, while in New York, he said that "God revealed Himself to me and it was such an experience of His love that I had to ask Him to stay His hand." Although Moody was seeing souls saved, it was this experience that changed him into the evangelist whom would be used by God in other countries as well as his own. It does not state that he spoke in tongues.

There are many other instances of some of the great men whom God has used down the centuries who described the baptism of the Holy Spirit in various ways. John Wesley called it the second blessing and referred to it as entire sanctification. He thought believers could be perfected and the sinful nature eradicated. I don't believe that, of course. Although it's a nice thought, there would be fewer problems in church life if that were the case! Nevertheless, they had encounters with the Holy Spirit after conversion which impacted them. Although the Wesleys did not speak in tongues, their experiences were very real. We should understand also that God never forces the individual to speak in tongues.

Instances recorded in the Bible were spontaneous, but they still demanded the willingness of the individual to speak in the supernatural utterances. The Bible records that, at Pentecost, "They all began to speak with tongues as the Spirit gave them utterance" (Acts 2:4). The utterance came from the Holy Spirit, and then they began to speak. It is our willingness and our voice, but the Holy Spirit gives the utterance. Both D. L. Moody and R. A. Torrey believed that the baptism of the Holy Spirit was a subsequent experience independent from that of conversion and was an empowering by the Spirit for service available for every believer in every age.

The Welsh revival, which began in 1904, only lasted under one year in duration under the leadership of Evan Roberts, a twenty-six-year-old former coal miner. However, in that time, one hundred thousand people were converted. Other revivals had preceded this which affected Roberts. His meetings were filled with singing, joy, and laughter but marked with the presence of God and the Holy Spirit's power to convict of sin and bring people to repentance and sal-

THE GOSPEL WE PREACH

vation. Although, again, there was no evidence that people spoke with tongues, it was a genuine revival. I share this to underline the fact that there was a definite spiritual awakening in various parts of the world.

At a Bible school ran by a man called Charles Parham in Topeka, Kansas, in 1901 and later in 1906 in Azusa Street in Los Angeles, California, under William Seymour's leadership, many people received the baptism in the Holy Spirit and spoke in tongues. Many were healed in those meetings, and the presence of God would literally appear as a cloud of glory at the Azusa Street meetings. The Holy Spirit was awakening His church to an empowering for service as Jesus had taught those early disciples prior to His ascension.

In 1902, a man called T. B. Barratt, who was born in England but had become a naturalized Norwegian at four years of age, planted a church in Oslo called the Oslo City Mission. In 1906, he was sent to America to raise funds for a large central mission in Oslo. While he was in his hotel room on October 7, although hundreds of miles away from the Azusa Street revival, he received the baptism in the Holy Spirit. He said, "I began to shout as loud as I could in a foreign language," and he also began singing in tongues. When he returned to Norway, he met opposition, as is often the case when the Holy Spirit is at work. His meetings were soon packed, and news spread to various countries.

Alexander Boddy, an Anglican vicar, heard about the revival and went over from Sunderland, England, to investigate what was happening. He heard children speaking in tongues and prophesying. He was convinced this was the Holy Spirit's work and invited T. B. Barrett over to his church in Sunderland. T. B. Barrett's Anglican Church was in debt for a new roof, but the story goes that the fire fell and burned up the debt. A stone is laid to this day with that inscription on it. There were two weeks of amazing meetings as people attended from near and far and were baptized in the Holy Spirit and started speaking in tongues.

News spread across the country and a man called Smith Wigglesworth decided to attend. He had heard that people were being

147

filled with the Holy Spirit and speaking in tongues. He was convinced he was already baptized in the Holy Spirit but had never spoken in tongues. Wigglesworth spent several days attending these meetings but becoming more and more desperate to speak in tongues. Before he left for his train home to Bradford, he walked to the vicarage.

A lady named Mrs. Boddy was in the library when Wigglesworth told her he wanted the tongues. Her reply was, "When you are baptized in the Holy Spirit, the tongues will follow." He protested again that he was baptized in the Holy Spirit. Mrs. Boddy laid hands upon him at his request, and the fire fell! He received a vision of an empty cross, and then a supernatural flow of tongues came with great joy and peace flooding his heart. Wigglesworth was never the same again. He was transformed and, eventually, moved into a ministry of his own, accompanied with great signs and wonders not only in Britain but across the world.

It was this empowering and baptism of the Holy Spirit that launched the early disciples into a bold witness with supernatural signs and wonders accompanying their ministry. They were embarking on a commission with a promise—"Greater works than these shall you do because I go to the Father" (John 14:12). When the Holy Spirit fell upon the one hundred and twenty in the upper room at Pentecost, they knew Jesus had not simply disappeared in a cloud when He ascended but He had actually reached the Father's throne. Peter, in his sermon that day, referred to Him as "this same Jesus" (Acts 2:36). The One who was declared to be Lord and Christ was the same Jesus who walked the shores of Galilee, who healed the sick and raised the dead. He had not changed; He is the same yesterday, today, and forever. The Gospels are full of miraculous healings and signs and wonders which followed Him wherever He went.

He healed lameness, palsy, paralysis, fevers, blindness, deafness and leprosy. He cast out demons and raised the dead. He healed a man with dropsy and a woman who had an issue of blood also Malchus's ear when Peter chopped it off with his sword! I don't think Peter was actually aiming for the ear but more like the soldier's head.

Either way, Jesus would have healed him! Jesus walked on water and fed thousands with a few loaves and fish. There was also the miraculous catch of fish and the calming of the storm. These were signs and wonders.

People may be able to try and explain away some healings, but it's difficult to deny the miraculous when confronted with the raising of Lazarus from the dead after four days of being in the tomb! The disciples had been witnesses of all these things. They were privileged to be in the greatest "signs and wonders" Bible school ever. Every day, there was something different; every day, there was a new challenge and new truth and often a different approach to healing and deliverance.

There were occasions when He spoke the word of healing as in the case of the centurion's servant who had been left at home sick (Matt. 8:5–13). Other times, He touched people, He rebuked sickness, and He prayed for people. He gave commands as He did with the man with the withered hand (Luke 6:6–10) and the paralytic (Mark 2:11). The woman with the issue of blood touched Him and was healed (Luke 8:42–48). He rebuked demons and cast them out (Mark 5). Sometimes, He had to get rid of certain people to perform a miracle as in the case of Jairus's daughter.

When Jesus came to the house where the young girl had died, He found many who were weeping and wailing. They ridiculed Him when He said she was just sleeping. Jesus had to clear the house of unbelief to make way for the miracle. It's interesting to note that Jesus could do no mighty works in His hometown except lay His hands on a few sick people and heal them. The problem again was unbelief on the part of His own hometown people. They knew Him as the carpenter's son and someone who grew up among them and were offended by Him. Jesus said to them, "A Prophet is not without honor except in his own country among his own relatives and in his own house" (Mark 6:1–6).

When there is an atmosphere of faith, miracles and healings can take place. If God's people gather with expectation, they create the kind of atmosphere that is pregnant with miracles. There is a great need today for faith to be preached and the expectation level to be raised because it is the miraculous ministry of signs and wonders, healings, and miracles that will still move towns cities and nations to faith in the living God.

Empowered by the Holy Spirit, the Spirit-filled believers soon began to see miracles taking place as they listened to the promptings of the Holy Spirit and sought His guidance as they evangelized Jerusalem, Judea, Samaria, and the known world.

The healing of the lame man in Acts 3 opened up Jerusalem and also caused a clash of kingdoms, with threats from the authorities not to teach and preach in the name of Jesus! The answer was a Spirit-filled prayer meeting where believers were further emboldened to preach the Gospel, and multitudes were added to the Church as they believed (Acts 5:15–16). People in the streets were being healed as Peter's shadow passed by.

Philip experienced healings and conversions as he preached in Samaria (Acts 8). Peter found a man who had been bedridden for eight years in Lydda, and he said, "Jesus Christ heals you get up and make your bed" (Acts 9:34). Immediately, he got up and made his bed! Paul and Barnabas were in Iconium and spoke boldly of the grace of God, and the Lord confirmed His Word with signs and wonders (Acts 14:1–4).

Again, this account bears witness to the fact that the devil does not like this kind of preaching with demonstrations of the Kingdom of God because the whole city was divided, some sided with the Jews and some with the apostles. When enemy territory is invaded, a battle pursues! The apostles fled the city to escape being stoned; and when they came to Lystra, they met a man who was crippled and had never walked from birth. He listened intently to the preaching, and Paul recognized he had faith to be healed and said with a loud voice, "Stand up straight on your feet!"

The man just didn't stand up; he leaped and walked. The people were so amazed that they believed the gods had come down to them.

Paul and Barnabas quickly stopped them from worshipping and sacrificing to them, telling them that they were only men but men with a message. The message was that they were to turn from idols to the living God. When Jews from Antioch came, things turned sour and, with their persuasive words, turned the multitudes against them. They stoned Paul and dragged him out of the city, thinking he was dead. The apostle wasn't finished yet!

The disciples gathered around him, and Paul rose up to continue in the ministry to which God had commissioned him. The one-time persecutor of the church was now on the receiving end of persecution, but nothing would deter him. He counted it an honor to suffer for Christ; and if in the process he was martyred, he knew he would immediately be in the presence of the Lord (Acts 14:8–20).

The demon-possessed slave girl was delivered when Paul and Silas went to Philippi (Acts 16:18). In the city of Ephesus, we have this remarkable account in Acts 19:11, and we read, "Now God worked unusual miracles by the hands of Paul." The King James Authorized Bible renders the word *unusual* as *special*. There are *healings, notable healings, miracles,* and *special miracles*. It was *special miracles* that occurred in Ephesus that led to such a revival. Special miracles stand in a class all of their own.

I remember reading of the account of the ministry of Stephen Jeffreys who was holding meetings in a town called Bishop, Auckland, in the northeast of England many years ago. A young woman called Celia Brown came to the meeting. Celia was totally blind due to the fact that she did not have any eyes, just sockets. The evangelist put his hands over her eyes; and immediately, God gave her a pair of lovely blue eyes.

Hundreds of people came to Christ through that special miracle. With special miracles, people either dismiss them outright and blatantly refuse to believe that such things could ever happen today or they have to admit this must be the power of God. Smith Wigglesworth, to whom I referred regarding his baptism in the Holy Spirit, raised several people from the dead, including his own wife!

Accounts of church growth occurred through the Book of Acts, and most related to signs and wonders. Miracles was definitely in the DNA of the early church. They looked for it and expected it, and it happened! I recall one of our lecturers in Bible college relating the story of how a group of students had gone out on ministry for the weekend; and on their return, he had asked them how many had been saved, filled with the Holy Spirit, and healed. They replied "None."

"Did you believe these things would happen?" the lecturer asked.

"Not really," they replied.

"Well then, you got what you believed for, didn't you?" he answered.

We have to believe what we are preaching and preach what we are believing for.

Questions may be asked regarding miracles and signs and wonders as to how those early disciples moved in such faith. The obvious answer is that they had received an encounter with God and the Holy Spirit that completely changed their lives. There is no substitute for an intimate relationship with the Lord and times when the infilling of the Holy Spirit takes place.

Paul's exhortation to the Ephesian believers was to be filled with the Holy Spirit, which really means "keep being filled and refilled" (Eph. 5:18). The baptism of the Holy Spirit not only changed and empowered them but opened up the door to the supernatural gifts of the Holy Spirit (1 Cor. 12:4–11). In the list, we find gifts of healings and working of miracles, and the Apostles recognized it was not by their own power but simply by these grace gifts of the Holy Spirit. Gifts are something we receive and do not earn; they always kept that in mind because just as the crowd wanted to hail Paul and Barnabas as gods because of the miracles, the apostles knew it was not their power but the gifts of the Holy Spirit at work (Acts 14:12).

The gift of faith is also in that list, which we see in operation at times when a command was given to rise from a sick bed or as Peter and John did with the lame man as they lifted him up from being sat at the gate of the temple (Acts 3). When the gift of faith is in operation, it supersedes ordinary faith as it is on a totally different level. The person operating this gift at that moment has no doubt of the outcome, of a command, or prayer that is made.

I personally have known times when this has happened as I have prayed for the sick; sometimes, it has operated when praying for people who were deaf. If they were wearing a hearing aid, when asking them to remove it from their ear, I have been so confident they would be healed I could have put the hearing aid on the floor and crushed it! Healings have taken place, and I have always resisted the temptation to crush the hearing aids!

Dreams, visions, words of knowledge and words of wisdom, healings and miracles, signs, and wonders are all there in the book of Acts; but they didn't end there! Shortly after I was saved, I began to seek the Lord for the baptism in the Holy Spirit. I read the scriptures and any magazine I could find that would help me to understand what this really was. I was prayed for a number of times but never spoke in tongues. The one thing I wanted was for this experience to be absolutely real and not something I had conjured up in my head. If the baptism in the Holy Spirit is real, then I wanted the real thing.

A spiritual thirst grew within my heart. I would tell the Lord how I felt and of my desire for the infilling of the Holy Spirit with the speaking in tongues. However, there was no way I was just going to say the first thing that popped into my head! Months passed by, and I grew more and more thirsty for the infilling of the Holy Spirit. I remember walking one evening and praying; and suddenly, I said out loud, "Tomorrow I am going to be filled with the Holy Spirit." I had no special plans for the next day as it was Easter weekend, but I decided I would go to a local Easter convention.

These were times when numbers of churches would gather together and guest speakers would be invited. I loved those times listening to the Word of God. Often in each meeting, there would be two preachers ministering the Word. I was sitting in the Saturday evening service, and it had just begun and the pastor led the congregation in prayer. As I was bowed in prayer, I suddenly began to quietly speak in other tongues. I was baptized in the Holy Spirit.

My heart leapt with great joy! The God of heaven had heard my cry and answered my prayer. The devil hates it when we receive anything from God and, a few days later, tried to tell me—through an insinuation in my mind—that all this speaking in tongues was just in my mind. I began to speak out loudly in tongues and said to the devil, "That's not in my mind!" It wasn't. He knew it, I knew it, and that settled it!

After two years in the Assemblies of God Bible College, I really felt called of God to the ministry of an evangelist. I received an invitation to assist with a town-wide evangelistic and divine healing crusade. (That's what we used to call them years ago, not *missions* but *crusades*.) I have the letter to this day from Pastor Ray Belfield inviting me for a period of some six—possibly, ten weeks—to help prepare for the crusade and do some follow-up and visiting of any new people who would make a decision for Christ.

I arrived in Wigan, Lancashire. I was twenty-two years of age, ready to help and eager to learn. The plan was that we would push flyers through just about every door in the town, advertise in the newspapers, and travel around the streets with a loudspeaker strapped to the top of the car, announcing the upcoming meetings. Special days of prayer and fasting also took place during this time of preparation. Although the church had a new building in a prime location in the town, there were probably around sixty people in all that attended regularly.

The pastor and his wife and family had an apartment over the church, and I slept in a little room downstairs next to the boiler room. (At least it was warm and I had my own room, which I never did at the Bible college as they were shared rooms.) I would pray in tongues for the meetings in that little room. Little did I know that I could be heard upstairs in the apartment. Just above my room was the kitchen and the Belfields had what we call in England a budgerigar, possibly called a canary in the USA. This bird was listening intently to me and began copying my speaking in tongues! No, I am not suggesting it was filled with the Holy Spirit! We laughed when we realized what had happened.

The time for the crusade to commence drew near, and the plan was to have a large tent erected that would seat approximately five hundred people in one part of the town for a week, then move it to another area of the town for another week, and for the final week, we would have meetings in the church building. The first week saw people testifying to being healed, and news began to spread around the town. The second week arrived, and we had moved the tent across the town. It was Monday evening and almost fifty yards away was a little bungalow (ranch), and outside was a young woman of approximately thirty years of age who was sat in a wheelchair.

When the time came for the evening meeting, her husband pushed her into the tent and right to the front row. He then left as he had no desire to stay for the meeting. The tent was comfortably full that night, and as the Evangelist Melvin Banks preached the Gospel many responded and made decisions for Christ. Then came the moment that would dramatically impact these meetings. First in line for prayer for healing was the young woman in the wheelchair.

As she was prayed for, she immediately rose from the wheelchair. She had been suffering not only from paralysis due to an accident but also angina, asthma, and epilepsy. She began walking around and then up and down the aisle in the tent. By that time, the atmosphere was charged with excitement and faith. Most of the people gathered were not used to church services. They shouted, clapped, whistled, and cheered some standing on the canvas chairs. I can only imagine those times were like some of the scenes in and around Galilee as Jesus healed the sick.

The Bible leaves us very often with just the facts; and we are left to imagine what the atmosphere and impact was as miracles took place and lepers were cleansed, cripples walked again, and the blind received their sight. Back in Wigan, crowds came night after night when news hit the town through the local newspaper, with a front-page picture of the young woman standing alongside her wheelchair, and the headlines read "Paralyzed mum walks again." Some nights, we would still be in the tent praying for the sick at midnight. One particular night, there were so many people pushing forward for prayer that suddenly, the evangelist asked some of them to form a line over to where I was standing so I could pray for them!

You may have heard the story of how the mother eagle will nudge her eaglets over the edge of the cliff when she thinks they are ready to fly. Well, this was my nudge! In no time, there was a long line of people waiting for me to pray for them. Some have asked, when I have related this story, whether or not I was nervous. I can't remember how I felt as it all happened so quickly, but what I do remember was the atmosphere was so pregnant with miracles and the presence of God that I felt I could believe for anything.

The first man in line stepped forward for me to pray for him. I asked him what he was suffering from, and he answered, "I am blind in one eye." I placed my hand over his blind eye, prayed a short prayer, and then removed my hand. "I can see," he said. "I can see!" Again, the atmosphere was so charged with faith that I don't think I was really surprised at all. That launched me into praying for the sick. I had been nudged over the cliff, and now I was learning to fly!

With over two thousand decisions recorded during that crusade, I stayed way beyond the possible ten weeks for which I had initially been invited. People needed to be visited and encouraged in their faith; so for the next year, I was out visiting those who registered decisions for Christ almost every day. The following year, we followed up with eight more tent crusades around the town, but this time I was the evangelist.

Hundreds of decisions for Christ again were recorded, and Pastor Ray Belfield decided he would hire double-decker buses (buses with a upstairs deck) to pick up people around the town who did not have their own transport in order to encourage them to come for the Sunday-evening meetings. He needed volunteers to become a hostess on the different bus routes. His wife, Barbara, was one; and my wife, Valerie (although at that time we were not dating), was one of the other volunteers.

She relates the following funny story: She had boarded the bus, and it was on its way around the route when she saw a group of ladies waiting at a certain bus stop. She rang the bell for the bus driver to stop and then quickly ushered them all on to the bus and off they went to the church. As the bus pulled up outside the church, some of the ladies were heard to say, "This doesn't look like the bingo hall, does it?" They were supposed to be playing bingo, but that night they all went into the church and heard the Gospel!

Maybe in heaven there could be some of those ladies who one day will remind us that they are so thankful they didn't make it to the bingo hall that night! It was the following year that I was asked to conduct an evangelistic crusade by the Assemblies of God Home Missions Department. Over the next five years, I would often be away on what we called "pioneer crusades." We would take a team of young people into a town where we were planning to plant a church and for three weeks hold meetings in a hired hall where I would preach the Gospel and pray for the sick.

During those meetings, and since as my wife Val and I have traveled to different countries, we have seen some wonderful healings and miracles take place as we have prayed for the sick. Allow me to give just a few testimonies.

I was preaching in England years ago, and the crusade meetings were being held in a school hall. I remember a couple who had traveled some twenty miles to get to the meeting, bringing their four-year-old daughter for prayer. They were Catholics but had heard about the meetings. Their daughter was in a wheelchair, and she didn't speak or really move. She was a pitiful sight. Her parents told me she had been given only weeks to live due to a brain tumor.

Each night, she slept at the bottom of their bed and often would vomit during the night. I prayed for her, and there was no visible change or inclination that any improvement had occurred. I encouraged the parents to believe and assured them we would continue to pray. It was just about one year later when I was back in the city of Coventry where the family actually lived that I was preaching at a local church in the city. Just before the meeting began, I was with the pastor in his office when there was knock on the door. One of the church elders walked in and told me there was a gentleman who would like to see me. He was shown into the office and introduced himself as the father of the little girl we had prayed for the previous year.

He told me that the very night they arrived home from the crusade meeting, they laid their daughter at the bottom of their bed as was their custom. At 3:00 a.m. that morning, their daughter woke and said "I am not going to die." From that time, he said she has gradually gotten better and he brought her to the church for us to see her. Down the aisle ran a five-year-old little girl who, one year before, was on the brink of death. Praise God for His miracle-working power.

I remember a ballerina coming to one of our meetings who had a collapsed lung. God wonderfully healed her. In those same meetings, a little girl with a twisted foot was healed. I prayed for a man who had suffered a stroke—his left arm paralyzed—and God set him instantly free. People suffering from cancer, epilepsy, slip disk, and many other ailments have been healed as hands have laid upon them in obedience to the Great Commission Jesus gave.

Recently, while ministering in Uganda, it seemed just about everyone in the prayer line received healing from the Lord. The first to be prayed for was a young woman who had what could be described as a frozen shoulder as she couldn't raise her left arm. After prayer, she was instantly healed; and she was so delighted, she rotated her arm time after time even when she went back to her seat! She was just overjoyed with her healing. That raised people's faith in the prayer line; and as my wife and I prayed, one after the other were testifying to being healed.

Everyone we have prayed for, of course, had not been healed. There may be a number of reasons why that has not taken place, but one thing I have learned is that we must not base our theology upon whether people are healed or not but upon what the Bible says.

Sometimes, as we have prayed for people and they have fallen to the floor, I don't look for this. I certainly don't suggest it to them, and I would never dream of pushing anyone down. Having said that, it sometimes occurs; but I am more interested in how people rise up as to whether they have been healed rather than the fact that they may have fallen down.

I often smile to myself when I think of the time when we were in England pastoring our first church in Ulverston, Cumbria. We were holding our Sunday meetings in the town hall due to the fact that we were in the midst of renovating an old concert hall built in 1850 into a Christian center, with a worship hall, restaurant, etc.

In the Sunday evening service, a young woman came out for prayer. She was quite tall and well built, and our two elders stood by her side as I prayed for her. They had their eyes closed, and so did I (bad idea). I was praying for a little while with my hand just lightly placed upon her forehead when I realized I could no longer feel her forehead! I opened my eyes to find that she was very slowly falling backward. By the time the two elders realized the same, she was now leaning backward at about forty-five degrees.

They quickly tried to catch her, and as they leaned forward, they both banged into each other's head. The outcome was the young woman lay on the floor completely oblivious to what had just happened, enjoying the blessing of God, while the two elders sat at either side of the aisle with their spectacles in their hands, holding their heads! When praying for the sick or possessed always, keep your eyes open. It helps to avoid what I have just described and also to discern what is happening as you are praying.

I know that falling down when prayed for is often criticized and there was a time when I myself was not sure what to think. However, that changed when my wife Val and I were at a camp meeting years ago and she was suffering with acute back pain. The preacher who knew us very well and also knew that we were quite skeptical of these things asked for people to come forward for prayer. As he prayed for Val, he felt her falling backward and thought, *You're not going to like this!* When she eventually got up, she was completely set free from back pain.

I have come to the conclusion that we must draw a distinction between the *manifestation* of the Holy Spirit and a *reaction* to the Holy Spirit. When a lightbulb is switched on, there is a manifestation of light; if there was no bulb and someone stuck their finger in the socket, there would be a reaction! (I don't advise that, of course.) When the Holy Spirit's presence is evident, sometimes, there are human reactions. These things have occurred down the centuries as people have been known to shake, fall down, weep, cry out, and dance under the power of God.

At Saul's conversion, he fell to the ground (Acts 9:4). Prophet Ezekiel fell on his face as he saw a vision (Ezek. 1:28). Daniel had the same reaction (Daniel 8:17). The soldiers fell to the ground when coming to arrest Jesus (John 18:6). Trembling and shaking came upon the people who were with Daniel as he saw a vision (Daniel 10:7). People trembled under conviction of sin, and some clung to the pillars of the building when Jonathon Edwards preached his famous sermon on July 8, 1741, entitled "Sinners in the Hands of an Angry God."

I stress, these are not manifestations of the Holy Spirit but, rather, human reactions. The thing we need to keep in mind is that while we walk by faith and not by sight or feelings, what God calls us into is a love relationship. With any relationship, it is not devoid of feelings; and I am not advocating some of the strange things that sometimes are reported, but we do need to feel His love and experience God. Otherwise, we simply have a cold, unemotional faith that soon becomes mere religion. As mentioned earlier, D. L. Moody experienced an outpouring of God's love, such that he had to ask God to stay His hand. He was obviously overcome with this outpouring.

Signs, wonders, and supernatural occurrences, as well as healings, are promised as we obey the command to preach the Gospel and are definitely a promise for the last days as Peter declared in his sermon at Pentecost. There should not be a cessation of supernatural manifestations but, rather, an experience of these things.

To return to the text mentioned at the beginning of this chapter, Mark 16:18, and the signs that would follow, one of which is "they will cast out demons." In this spiritual warfare, the apostle Paul tells us this:

> We do not fight against flesh and blood but against principalities, against powers, against the rulers of the darkness of this age, against spiritual hosts of wickedness in the heavenly places. (Eph. 6:12)

Many people believe that demons are fallen angels, although the Bible does not specifically say this. There are scriptures which allude to the fact that when the devil rebelled against the Most High God, he was cast out of God's presence and a number of angels followed him. Some of the passages refer to these angels as having sinned (2 Pet. 2:4). Also Jude 1:6 makes mentions of these angels, saying they "did not keep their proper domain but left their own abode."

We know, of course, that these evil spirits are active in the world today as they were in New Testament times. Jesus did not seek evil spirits; they found Him. He did not teach on their origin, but He did cast them out and recognized that they were responsible for many of the afflictions He cured.

Before I list a number of these instances, please don't misinterpret what I want you to understand. While the root cause in many of the sicknesses and diseases Jesus dealt with was demonic—and He had to cast out the demon—this does not mean that every similar sickness or disease has the same root cause. In Mark 9:32, there was a man who was dumb, but when the demon was cast out, he was able to speak. On another occasion, He came across a boy who had convulsions. He would foam from the mouth as the spirit would seize him. Jesus rebuked the unclean spirit and healed the boy (Luke 9:42). In Luke 9:2, Jesus "gave His disciples power and authority over all demons and to cure diseases."

Luke records in the book of the Acts of the Apostles that "Jesus went about doing good and healing all who were oppressed of the devil for God was with Him" (Acts 10:38). From this verse, we can conclude that all sickness is an oppression of the devil. However, we must draw a distinction between the terms used such as *oppression* and *possession*. It seems clear that the man who Jesus met in the country of the Gadarenes was clearly possessed by many demons (Mark 5:2). No one could keep him bound; even with chains, he was completely taken over by demons.

It is rare we come across this kind of possession, but it does exist. I heard a true story of a team that went to preach the Gospel in a village in Africa. When they arrived, the villagers did not want to know; they had heard before but were not convinced; but then they told the missionary team that there was a man who lived in the woods who was completely insane and no one could help him. They said, "If you can deliver that man and bring him back to a sound mind, we will believe the Gospel you preach."

The team went in search of the man; they found him in the woods; and he had long, matted hair and long fingernails and was obviously possessed by demons. The team commanded the demons to depart, and the man came back to sanity. They brought him back to the village where he washed and got cleaned up. The result was, forty people in the village got saved, and that man now is the pastor of a church in Uganda.

With some of the references mentioned to the casting out of demons, often, this is oppression by an evil spirit that is at the root of the sickness and needs to be cast out before healing can take place. Whereas in a possession, an evil spirit has complete control of the person. There is a balance in all these things, and we have to be careful that we do not get obsessed with evil spirits and see them as the problem behind everything. When Paul and Silas were in the city pf

Ephesus, it was the young slave girl who kept following them and she was possessed by a spirit of divination and was crying out that they were servants of the Most High God (Acts 16:16).

She did this for many days until Paul, who became greatly annoyed, turned and cast out the evil spirit. Of course, this caused uproar in the city and eventually led them to being imprisoned and the jailor getting saved! The point I am making is that Paul, like Jesus, did not go out searching for evil spirits; they found him. And when they did, like Jesus, Paul dealt with them.

Keep in mind this passage: "In My name they will cast out demons, they will speak with new tongues, they will take up serpents" (Mark 16:17–18).

Having dealt with the first two signs, we will now look at the "taking up of serpents" and the "drinking of any deadly thing" with the promise they will not be harmed.

You may have heard reports in some churches where they literally bring snakes to the service and the preacher picks them up. The sad facts are that some died from snakebites while others survived. I don't believe for one minute that God intended us to literally take up serpents and to make a show or try and prove a point.

If Jesus didn't go around looking for evil spirits, then I'm sure he wouldn't have encouraged His disciples to go looking for snakes! The one occasion where a snake coiled itself around Paul was when he was on the aisle of Malta (Acts 28:4–5). Paul simply shook it off and suffered no ill effect. I think Jesus was making the point, as the disciples were commissioned, whether snakes or poison, there was a promise of protection.

I remember years ago, a missionary called Harry Dring coming to the church in Wigan, Lancashire, England. He had been a missionary to Argentina for many years—in fact, when he left the shores of England as a young man, his sisters waved him off as the ship set sail. He would not see them again for another twenty-five years. I think that was his first furlough. I have often thought of those early missionaries who had no cell phones or internet and to mail a letter, it would take months to arrive. And yet, they went in the will of God, no sacrifice being too great.

He related a story in the church that night rather matter-of-factly as though it was no big deal, but it left me wide-eyed with amazement. He told us that one day as he was riding through the bush in Argentina, a snake reared up and bit him on the leg. "I just took out my knife, cut the leg where the bite was, and carried on, with no ill effects," he said.

We live in days of great challenge. May men and women rise up and believe the Word of God again and dare to preach this glorious Gospel with signs following.

This is the Gospel we preach.

15

Preaching the Gospel
with the Holy Spirit

In 1 Peter 1:12, we find this phrase regarding the preaching of the Gospel with the Holy Spirit sent down from heaven. Peter is encouraging the believers and teaching them that the salvation they have experienced is what prophets spoke of hundreds of years before. While the prophets did not fully understand what they were prophesying, they desired to know. The revelation came to them by the Holy Spirit, the same Holy Spirit that now had accompanied the word of the Gospel that these believers had received.

I think this is an amazing truth and the greatest privilege we can be afforded, not only to simply hear the Gospel but to be called to preach it. I am sure there is something in this phrase that is a dynamic truth that is often missed. When anyone stands to preach this glorious message, it can have eternal consequences. And when the preacher can say as Jesus did when He stood up in the synagogue in Nazareth—"The Spirit of the Lord is upon Me because He has anointed Me to preach the Gospel" (Luke 4:18)—hearts will be touched, lives changed, souls saved, and to those who refuse the message, they will leave with conviction etched upon their hearts.

There is a difference between just preaching and preaching with the Holy Spirit. By that I mean, things happen when the preacher is full of the Holy Spirit. He is the Spirit of revelation and wisdom.

He is the Spirit of Truth, and He is the One who Jesus said would be alongside the disciples and would dwell within them. Paul encouraged the believers in the church at Ephesus to "be filled with the Spirit" (Eph. 5:18), which really means to be being filled with the Holy Spirit.

We live in a world where many things depend on batteries. Many of kids' toys are battery operated. When our boys used to open their presents at Christmas, I would be counting how many batteries would be needed! Clocks run on batteries, our vehicles need batteries. It's never a good time when the battery in the car runs flat, and it always seems to be the wrong time. I now have acquired a little gadget that is not much bigger than a cell phone that I can carry in the car, and if the battery runs flat, this gadget will boost the battery and get the car started!

Batteries are good but they can run flat. Our spiritual batteries can also run flat. Normally, car batteries are prone to run flat in the middle of winter when the heater is on full, the wiper blades are going, and full headlights are needed. When too many things are draining the battery, the battery can easily get run down. Every believer and every Gospel preacher must make sure they don't run on empty.

It can happen to anyone. It can also happen to those who seem to be most successful. They can drift in autopilot but without the compassion of God working through them. Too often it is because they have become too busy, schedules become full, and the preacher, whose main priority is to prepare to preach with the Holy Spirit sent down from heaven, sometimes stands before a congregation whose needs are numerous. He smiles and gets through his sermon, but he knows in his heart of hearts that his spiritual battery is flat.

If this situation is not rectified, it becomes noticeable by others. God never intended us to preach the Gospel on our own but with our coworker, the Holy Spirit. As the congregation gathers, it is the Holy Spirit who knows every heart and every need represented on each occasion. He can move upon the heart of the preacher, who is full of the Spirit, and drop words of knowledge and inspiration that brings revelation to the hearers.

It is said of Stephen, the first Christian martyr, that "he being full of the Holy Spirit, gazed into heaven and saw the Son of Man standing at the right hand of God" (Acts 7:55). The Spirit-filled preacher will always have Christ at the center of his message, and his message will always impact his hearers. When Stephen nailed sin to the doors of the hearts of his hearers, they were cut to the heart (Acts 7:51–54). The Holy Spirit is the Spirit who brings conviction of sin; without it, there can be no repentance. However, the Spirit-filled preacher must be bold enough to expose what sin is.

Conviction must precede conversion. Sin must be owned before salvation can be received. It is the Holy Spirit who exposes the hidden sins of the heart, the impure motives, the pride that refuses to bow at the cross. The prodigal son had to "come to himself" to see the plight he was in before he turned homeward. The Holy Spirit, working through the Spirit-filled preacher with an anointed message, will point sinners homeward. He will show them the filth and degradation of their unbelieving hearts but will lead then back to a loving and forgiving Father.

The preacher must make continual checks on the measure of the Holy Spirit he is operating under. Recharging only happens in His presence. The prayer meeting in Acts 4 was a recharging of boldness and passion to take the message to the lost people of Jerusalem. The people knew these preachers had been with Jesus. The preacher of the Gospel is in touch with another world, and he must continually "taste of the power of the age to come" (Heb. 6:5). This old world drags people into its mold and leaves them with no hope at the end of life; but the preacher of the Gospel stands before them as a representative of another Kingdom, and he must make sure the presence of the King by the Holy Spirit is with him.

When the apostle Paul was saying farewell to the elders of the church from Ephesus, he told them to "take heed to themselves and to the church that the Holy Spirit had made them overseers" (Acts 20:28).

The secret place of the Most High, the intimate fellowship of times alone with the Lord when schedules are not allowed to interrupt, become times when a meeting takes place. This is not a meeting with people gathered but a meeting where two people gather—the preacher and the Lord. This is where the preacher has to become acquainted with His voice, His presence, and bathe in His love. The place where the Word of God is put into his heart and where God's promises are underlined with His presence. It's a place of transformation and change, a place of renewal where the soul and the spirit are recharged where peace reigns and faith is fueled.

Many have been the times when the Word of the Lord has come to me in the quiet place, reassuring me of His promises, pushing doubt from my mind, and filling me again with His Holy Spirit. The ministry can be draining at times; it can be demanding. I laugh to myself sometimes when people have said to me regarding Christmastime that this is my busiest time of the year.

Every day can be busy, but busyness must not be allowed to erode the secret place. Psalm 91 contains many wonderful promises, but the secret is the secret place. How can it be a secret place when we have it openly talked about here in this Psalm? The answer, of course, is quite simple. You could give a map to someone detailing every turn and every detail on the road to find what may be called secret treasure. Unless the person who receives the map makes the journey, they never find the treasure!

The first verse of this Psalm is the map, "He who dwells in the secret place of the Most High shall abide under the shadow of the Almighty" (Ps. 91:1). That's it—simple yet profound. There is nothing complicated. There are no roadblocks along the way that God places there, and the only roadblocks are the ones of our own making like busyness or lack of self-discipline.

If we can only get to the first verse and do it, the rest of the Psalm is full of treasure promises. The second verse is a confession of faith which comes from being in the secret place—"I will say of the Lord He is my refuge and my fortress; my God, in Him will I trust" (Ps. 91:2).

The preacher of the Gospel needs faith; without it, we cannot please God. When the message is preached, the preacher must stand in faith and deliver it without fear, believing that God will honor His Word. Results are not always immediate as it is like sowing seed. It has to germinate and be watered, but the preacher must know in his or her heart that what has been spoken are the words of eternal life and allow the coworker—the Holy Spirit—to apply and follow up in the hearts of the hearers.

When in the secret place, faith grows and the discovery that the Lord is your fortress and refuge becomes your confession. The secret is not just being in His presence (the secret place) but abiding or dwelling. There are times when we do need to come aside from all distractions, and we also need to understand that we cannot be locked away in some prayer closet all day. Jesus Himself walked everywhere or took a boat, and there were times when He withdrew Himself from the crowds. However, on other times, He was in their midst meeting needs. There were times when Paul was making tents to support himself and other times when he too could be alone. The secret is cultivating a relationship with the Lord at all times, or as Paul puts it, "Pray without ceasing." The secret place is not a closet or special room—it's a place in our heart.

To abide or dwell in that place, we have to make sure that nothing hinders His presence, no lurking sin or wrong thoughts. There is no room to harbor unforgiveness or bitterness or allow the enemy any access to any area of our lives. This is really where the battle takes place to "dwell in the secret place." Many believers have tasted and experienced the presence of the Lord but then fail to maintain it. It's like visiting someone in their house and then leaving. You had a nice visit, but you don't live there! Sadly, that is the experience of so many, even though the "secret place" is available all the time. The psalmist is really saying, "It's open house all the time."

In our first church, we lived in a neighborhood where many of the people who came to our church lived nearby. We have always said to the congregation wherever we have lived, "Our house is open house. You don't have to be invited to come and visit. You are always welcome." I think our neighbor was dizzy some days just watching people come and go as they literally popped in to see us as they passed by.

In another part of the country, the congregation—although they had the same invitation—didn't often do that. Our relationships were fine, but maybe it was the location where we lived or even a little cultural difference. As far as coming to the house uninvited is concerned, it was very infrequent. The psalmist is not, however, encouraging visits either frequently or infrequently but, rather, *dwelling*. That is the big difference, and that is the secret!

To preach with the Holy Spirit sent down from heaven is to preach with some fire. By that, I am not suggesting that the preacher has to be demonstrative or shout. I remember when I was first saved, we used to have a preacher come to the village church I attended from time to time, and I would sit in amazement at the delivery of his message. After the first sentence or so, he would then raise his voice to a certain pitch and never came back down until he had finished. It was hard to listen to because I felt I wanted to take a breath for the preacher!

Others think they haven't really preached a good sermon unless they have worked up a sweat. While yet others are so dreary, they nearly fall asleep before the congregation does! I can get excited with what I preach. After all, if I don't, there probably is not much hope of anyone else being excited; however, the delivery of the message is very important. Variety and the change of tone in the voice will keep people attentive.

Having said that, whatever our style of preaching is, every preacher needs the fire of God upon His words. John the Baptist spoke of the One who was to come (Jesus) who would baptize in the Holy Spirit and "fire."

The writer of the book of Hebrews describes the angels of God: "And of the angels He says: 'Who makes His angels spirits and His ministers a flame of fire'" (Heb. 1:7). This is referring to the supremacy of Christ as the Son of God over all created beings. The angels are His servants and do His bidding and are described as "ministers who are as flames of fire."

As preachers of the Gospel, we really need the fire of God upon us. By this I mean that our words will burn with the power and passion of God into the hearts of our hearers.

There is something attractive about fire. Have you watched a little child when it sees the flames of an open fire? Our little grandson Joey will go to the electric fire and switch it on whenever he comes 'round to our house; he is intrigued by the flame effect. Animals are attracted by fire. One reason is that they like to keep warm. We had a Labrador years ago and he would lie in front of the electric fire when there was only the glow of the flames flickering and heat wasn't on! Psychologically, he thought he was warmer as he lay there.

I remember many years ago when we were planting a church on the edge of the English Lake District in a small market town called Ulverston, we fortunately averted a house fire by just a few minutes. It was Easter Sunday morning; I had left for Church early along with our youth pastor as my wife intended to join us later, with our two boys, in time for the morning meeting to commence. I was facing the congregation and leading them in a good old Easter hymn. There was excitement among the people as we celebrated the resurrection of Christ.

Partway through the hymn, I noticed some commotion at the back of the church; and one of the elders walked up the aisle to explain that there was a house on fire. By this time, we had all stopped singing; and I made the announcement that someone's house was on fire. I had no idea whose house it was and calmly said, "OK, now let's sing verse 3." We started the next verse, and still there seemed to be a number of the people at the back of the hall walking in and out and one had grabbed a fire extinguisher off the wall. I also noticed my wife rushing out of the meeting. The elder of the church came walking down to the front and whispered in my ear, "It's your house that's on fire!"

I remember this incident vividly, and as calm as anything, I made another announcement, "Oh, it's our house that's on fire. Verse 4." I figured, if the house is on fire, there was nothing I can do at that moment; and luckily, the fire service had already been alerted by our neighbor. He had then driven to our church to alert us. By the way, that was the first time I had seen him in our church! I calmly announced again to the congregation, "Let's sing the next verse."

My wife relates the story that as one of the guys in the church drove her quickly to the house where the street was lined with children, fire trucks, and police. As part of our outreach efforts, we were holding a kids' Good News club every Monday evening in the school in the neighborhood. We would have over a hundred kids coming each week, and they all wore badges with their names on which showed they were members of the Good News club. They liked these badges so much that many of them wore them when they went to school. Because of this, we were well known in the neighborhood. Some of those kids who attended are now adults who have kept their faith in Jesus over the years.

When my wife got out of the car on the street, there was a chorus of voices that shouted, "Mrs. Tipple, your house is on fire!" The fireman took the door key from my wife and could see before he entered that the cooker had a pan on top that was smoking. The pan had oil in it that was used for cooking chips, as we English would say, otherwise known as French fries. The grill where we would toast bread, which was situated directly under the top of the cooker, had been left on from breakfast, and gradually the heat had warmed the oil until it was about to burst into flames. The fire officer was able to remove it only moments before flames erupted.

The kitchen and living room was full of black smoke, and it was this that had alerted our neighbor. Well, I have to confess, it wasn't me that left the grill on or my wife or one of our boys. It must have been the young man who was living with us at that time, our youth pastor who will not be named. Although when our paths cross from time to time, we often laugh about this incident though it wasn't funny at the time! We definitely had a crowd that day because of the fire!

To preach the Gospel with the Holy Spirit sent down from heaven will always cause a stir; for Stephen, hell was so stirred up that the people motivated by demons stoned him (Acts 7)! When people hear the Gospel preached this way, there will always be conviction of sin. The Holy Spirit will make bare their hearts, and they will see their sin.

The problem comes, of course, when people see the extent of their sin and do not want to deal with it. They will not enjoy the experience, but it will cause them to act mostly in one of two ways—they will either own it and turn to Christ and acknowledge that He took it upon Himself when He died upon the cross or they will rebel and reject, which often is displayed in anger or a decision to never darken the doors of the church again!

However, as pointed out in an earlier chapter, the Gospel has a magnetism all on its own. It can offend and yet still draw sinners to the cross and forgiveness. The Holy Spirit will always work with the Word of God and is our coworker and helper. May everyone who stands to minister this glorious Gospel be constantly aware that this is an awesome privilege and responsibility. Dwell in the secret place. Be filled with His Spirit and fire and preach this Gospel as though it may be the last time your hearers will have the chance to repent and be saved.

I remember years ago I was ministering in a town-wide evangelistic crusade in Droitwich, UK. The title of my message was "Things That Will Happen in a Moment of Time." I referred to the second coming of Jesus Christ and the resurrection of the dead. Shortly before the meeting began, I received a telephone call from my dad telling me that my mother was very ill and would probably not live for much more than twenty-four hours. I was committed to preaching that night and praying for the sick, but my plan was to drive across the country as soon as the meeting was over. Someone kindly loaned me the use of their car as at that time I didn't own one.

I drove over to my parents, arriving just before midnight to find that my mother had died a few hours earlier. The only consolation in all of this was that she had been saved a few years earlier, and we knew she had gone to be with the Lord and was now free from her suffering. During the week prior to the funeral, relatives came to visit us to pay their condolences. I remember speaking with my mother's cousin-in-law. He hadn't seen me for a few years, and he asked me what I was doing since I had left Bible college. I told him of the crusades and that I was working with the church in Wigan and that all this had resulted from my own conversion to Christ some years earlier. He listened to my story that day.

The funeral was due to take place on the Monday afternoon at 1:30 p.m. He and his wife attended the funeral with many other friends and relatives. The pastor leaned over the pulpit and pointed to the coffin and said quite bluntly, "Whether we like it or not, each one of us will have to go the same way unless Jesus comes first, for it is appointed unto man once to die and after that the judgment." I must admit, I had never heard anyone be so forthright at a funeral; but it was the truth and he preached it that day.

Exactly one week later, my dad and I were attending another funeral in another church just a few miles away at 1:30 p.m. This time, it was the funeral of my mother's second cousin who had talked with me the previous week! He was only forty years of age. Earlier that week, he had woken to go to his work and, on getting out of bed, had a heart attack. He died before he was able to reach the hospital. His body was laid in the next grave to my mother's.

It was within a few weeks of these funerals that I heard of one of my schoolboy friends, who had grown up in the same village as me and had played football with me in the school team, had died. He also liked to play cricket; and while playing for a local team on the village green, he was batting and his team needed only one run to win the game. He hit the ball and ran to make the winning run, only to collapse as he reached the other wicket crease. He was dead upon arrival at the hospital at just twenty-four years of age! With just weeks in between these three deaths, God impressed upon me the brevity of life.

As people listen to the Gospel with all its power, promises of forgiveness, and blessings, along with its warnings, we never know whether they will get another chance to respond and neither do they. Preach it with the love and compassion of Christ along with the Holy Spirit sent down from heaven and believe for great results.

This is the Gospel we preach.

"Give me the love that leads the way,
The faith that nothing can dismay,
The hope no disappointments tire,
The passion that will burn like fire,
Let me not sin to be a clod;
Make me thy fuel, Flame of God."
—Amy Wilson Carmichael

16

The Gospel and Hard Places

Every preacher will have heard this saying at some time or other, especially when venturing into a new area, taking on a new challenge either by planting a church or becoming the pastor of an existing one: "It's a hard place. You know, others have tried and not been successful." They are not the most encouraging words a preacher wants to hear when he may be moving his family across country or onto foreign soil, seeking to believe God for financial support and taking a faith step into a brand-new challenge.

When my wife and I felt the call of God to leave the church in Wigan and move to the small market town of Ulverston in Cumbria to plant a church, a pastor's wife said, "I don't know whether to be happy for you or to cry." Fortunately, that didn't deter us. We went and, by the grace of God, saw a church planted and then that church become a mother church to the church in Barrow-in-Furness, Cumbria—a town of some nine miles away.

There were tough times and battles, there was enemy resistance, especially in the first twelve months of being there, but I remember a time bowed in prayer in the little church building that we had at that time. With no one else around, I began to read from the prophecy of Isaiah from the Living Bible Translation. "When the Lord shall enlarge you" was a phrase that seemed to burn itself upon my heart.

I rose from my knees, saying, "God it's not *if* You will enlarge us but *when*. It's just a matter of time before You do it." Faith comes by hearing the Word of God, and faith definitely came to me that day. The situations that seemed to prevail at that time became in my mind and heart simply temporary. Better days were coming! Better days certainly did come as we began to see people turning to Christ and the church beginning to grow.

I think it is worthy of consideration also to ask the question *What is success?* Is success measured by the number of seats filled on any given Sunday? Is success measured by the size of building or the amount in the offering? Sadly, that is what many deem as success. I often wonder what the judgment seat of Christ will be really like when every believer and every preacher stands before the Lord to have their works rewarded and possibly some of those works burned up!

Please don't misinterpret the point I am making. Every Pastor wants to see their church grow, and thank God for churches that number in their thousands, but we need to thank Him also for the ones that maybe haven't seen the same amount of growth but nevertheless have maintained a testimony in their communities and the pastors who have remained faithful to their calling.

The book of the Revelation gives us a little insight as to how the Lord views His church. We have the account of the seven churches to which Jesus sends a message. Interestingly, He never refers to numbers and how many are attending! He reproves and He also commends. He deals with doctrine and immorality, false teachers, and faithfulness, among other things, but never mentions numbers. The one church that seemed to have it all by way of finances and wealth insomuch that they felt they had need of nothing was the church of the Laodiceans. And yet, Jesus was standing outside the door. He wasn't even in their midst! This church was diagnosed as being wretched, miserable, poor, blind, and naked (Rev. 3:17).

There are megachurches that have seen great increase in membership, kept the faith, preached the whole counsel of God, and have Jesus in their midst as the supreme attraction. On the other hand, there are small churches that maybe have struggled and have allowed all kinds of things to take the place of the passion for souls and the true worship of Christ. Big or small, it's not about numbers! Faithfulness to the calling of God is success.

But are there some places that are harder than others?

I would have to say "Yes, there are." Communities are different one from the other. It may be more difficult in wealthy, upper-class communities to penetrate them with the Gospel by virtue of the fact that these people may feel they have it all and don't need anything. But these communities are not out of reach as they still have their needs. Wealth doesn't guarantee a happy marriage or problem-free children. It does not guarantee good health and a life free from sickness. These areas are being penetrated by need-orientated evangelism—divorce care groups, grief groups, recovery groups, and more.

If the church dares to pray and believe for the sick to be healed, there can be breakthrough in these areas in the supernatural. Perhaps you live in that kind of area; and if you do, there is a strategy to reach it. Pray and allow the Holy Spirit to show you what you can do. Don't give up and believe the lie of the devil that this place is too hard!

Having said that, it was the common people who seemed to follow Jesus and be more open to His message. Communities where there is less wealth may be more open to the Gospel. There are countries that are more open than others. Some may be filled with idolatry and false religions, but Paul came up against all these things and still planted churches. We must take the words of Jesus to heart and believe them and, at the same time, resist the lie of the devil.

Jesus declared, "The fields are white unto harvest" (John 4:35), but I want you to notice something in this verse that is very important. Before Jesus said those words, He said this: "Behold I say to you lift up your eyes and look at the fields, for they are already white for harvest."

The first thing He said was to "lift up our eyes." We have to get our vision fixed on the whitened harvest and to take our eyes off

178

what may not be happening which has the habit of sapping faith and bringing a spirit of depression. People often use the term when someone is a little depressed and that "they are feeling down."

When someone is feeling that way, their head drops, their vision is earthbound, and they are looking at the ground in front of them instead of the fields in the distance, ready for reaping. We have to see the fields first before we can reap. Our vision has to be corrected, and we have to allow the one who the psalmist says is the "lifter of our heads" to raise our vision so that we see as He sees and refuse to believe the devil's lies that this place is too hard. Remember, Jesus was in Samaria when He said these things; and at that time, the Jews had no dealings with the Samaritans yet a whole city of men came out to hear Him!

I want also to draw your attention back to the book of Revelation and the church in Pergamos:

> And to the angel of the church in Pergamos write, "These things says He who has a sharp two-edged sword; I know your works and where you dwell, where Satan's throne is. And you hold fast to My name and did not deny My faith even in the days in which Antipas My faithful martyr, who was killed among you, where Satan dwells." (Rev. 2:12–13)

Pergamos became the chief town of a new province of Asia. It also had the first temple of the Caesar cult erected to Rome and Augustus in 29 BC. A later shrine was erected to Trajan, and they also had the worship of Asklepios and Zeus, the symbol of Asklepios being that of a serpent. On a crag above Pergamos was an altar like a throne to Zeus. There were decorations of false gods and giants, the giants being portrayed as monsters with tails like serpents. This was to represent the conflict of the gods and the giants. Zeus was also called "Zeus the savior." Pergamos was an ancient seat of culture but thoroughly pagan.

Jesus described it as a place where Satan's throne is!

Believe it or not, there was a church planted there! If ever there was a "hard place," this was it!

We see idolatry pagan worship, monsters pictured with serpent like tails, shrines, and an altar to Zeus, who was called a savior. If this was not bad enough, a man called Antipas had been martyred and he is mentioned as a faithful witness. Church tradition says that he was a physician suspected of secretly propagating Christianity. He was accused of disloyalty to Caesar by members of the medical guild and was placed inside a copper bull. This was then heated over a fire until it was red hot. Who would like to volunteer for a church plant in this city?

It is interesting that it is called the place where Satan's throne is. Paul tells us that we wrestle against principalities and powers and spiritual wickedness in high places, but this was where Satan had set up his throne! There was definitely demonic resistance here. The church was not perfect—it had its problems, and things that needed to be put right—but nevertheless, there was a church. If Antipas was instrumental in planting this church, I'm sure he is in for a great reward. There are churches in the darkest places, and there are even underground churches. The Gospel has penetrated the hardest of places down the years. Thank God for faithful servants who sometimes labored many years before seeing a soul saved!

It was seven years before the missionary Carey baptized his first convert in India and seven years before Judson won his first disciple in Burma. Sometimes, men and women have labored faithfully without seeing much fruit for their labors; yet years later, a harvest was reaped by others. God's servants must always remind themselves that most of the time, we are entering into someone else's labors. The seed of the Word of God having been sown years before and watered over time suddenly springs to birth.

The Christian world looks on and sees the evangelist or pastor who seems to get immediate results; and often, little realize the prayers, labors of love, and faithfulness that others have made. I am convinced all will be revealed at the judgment seat of Christ when He hands out the rewards. Nothing goes unnoticed, heaven sees all things, and God rewards in His time.

Hard places can be moved by the Gospel even if Satan's throne is there. We have to believe that, ultimately, victory was won at the cross and the devil was defeated. He still has territory that he doesn't want to give up and will resist, but every believer must recognize the authority and power they have in Christ.

The apostle Paul went through many hardships and trials taking the Gospel into virgin territory. He bore in his body the marks of the beatings where the rod had coursed through his skin, the scars where rocks had hit his body when being stoned. If anyone could testify to planting churches in hard places, it was Paul. And yet this man knew that if God could open his hardened heart, He could do it with anyone.

He reminded the Ephesian church that they were once slaves to sin and under the devil's dominion (Eph. 2:1–3). With this constantly in mind, Paul pressed on, determined to preach the Gospel. If Paul was received and his message was received, he would plant a church and ordain elders. If his message wasn't received, he moved on to another city or town. He met idolatry, demon worship, pagan shrines, and sometimes hostile crowds; but wherever they would listen, Paul preached the Gospel, believing that hard places could be changed with the life-giving and soul-saving message of the Christ who had saved Him.

Ephesus was no easy place with its worship of the goddess Diana. The city was in uproar because of the revival, and Paul despaired for his life when he was in danger of going in to the amphitheater to a frenzied, demon-inspired crowd (Acts 19:28–34; 2 Cor. 1:8–9). The city of Corinth was not easy either, but God assured Paul that he had many souls in that city. It was later when Paul had planted the church and wrote to them that he reminded them of what some of them had been—fornicators, idolaters, adulterers, homosexuals, sodomites, thieves, covetous, drunkards, revilers, and extortioners (1 Cor. 6:11).

Thessalonica was a hard place too; Paul could only stay three Sabbath days because there was uproar from the Jews in that city. They claimed that Paul and his colleagues were proclaiming there was another king, Jesus, which was contrary to the decree of Caesar. Paul had to leave quickly, but he left a church behind (Acts 17:1–10)! By the way, the other thing that was said about Paul and his team was, "These who have turned the world upside down have come here too" (Acts 17:6). Hard places can be turned upside down!

They were fearless in spreading the Gospel; they believed for signs and wonders; and they prayed fervently for the towns and cities they were entering, knowing that there would be enemy resistance because they were entering enemy territory and announcing another kingdom.

I am aware that the apostle Paul taught us, "We wrestle not against flesh and blood but against principalities, against powers, against the rulers of the darkness of this age against spiritual hosts of wickedness in heavenly places" (Eph. 6:12). The question I pose is, *How did they pray against these powers?*

Over the years, I have heard differing accounts of how we should deal with this resistance from spiritual powers. Some believe that we should bind these powers in prayer. With that in mind, I have heard prayers like this: "I bind the spirit of adultery over this area or of suicide or …" If it was as easy as that, there would be no problems that couldn't be taken care of within a few minutes by one of these prayers. Now, I understand that we can all do things and pray things. Sometimes, that may not be the correct way, and God looks and sees faith and sincerity and can give us breakthroughs in areas that we are praying over.

However, those kinds of prayers I do not find through the book of Acts or taught in the Epistles. When Peter and John were forbidden to teach and preach again in the name of Jesus in Jerusalem, they went back to the community of believers and they all prayed. They didn't bind anything; rather, they asked for great boldness and signs and wonders to accompany the Word of God. Thousands were saved shortly after that.

There was no one shouting "I bind the spirit of religion over this city." I have come to the conclusion that intercession is wrestling against the powers that resist. It is the wrestling of faith and perseverance praying to the Father in the name of Jesus and then heaven coming to our aid with angels that war on our behalf. When he set himself to pray and intercede, Daniel was a captive who, in his teens, had been carried off to Babylon. It is while in captivity that Daniel received visions and dreams. In the tenth chapter, Daniel begins to pray fervently, eating no pleasant food—probably what we call a partial fast—but he had set his heart to understand what God would do in the last days and to humble himself before God.

In Daniel 10:12–21, we have insight into the fact that there are powerful territorial spirits such as the prince of Persia (Dan. 10:13). These powers are assigned by the devil to control nations, communities, etc. They work on the minds of men and women, they can influence decisions that are made politically, and they can influence culture and morals. These are evil powers set against the Gospel and churches that want to spread the Good News. Daniel was praying for twenty-one days, with no idea what was taking place in the heavenly realms.

The point I am making is simply this: as Daniel prayed and his answer was resisted, God sent an angel; and even this angel had to have help from Michael—an archangel—to fight in the heavenly realms and to bring the answer back to earth. Daniel was praying, and angels were fighting on his behalf! The powers of darkness will resist, but we must persist! As we do, the Greater One will send angels, if needed, to bring the answers to prayer.

The two main passages taught in the New Testament regarding "binding and loosing" and "binding the strong man" are found in Matthew 12:22–30 and Matthew 18:15–20.

In the first passage mentioned, Jesus is being accused of casting out demons by Beelzebub, the ruler of the demons. Jesus had just healed a man who was blind and mute. The Pharisees assumed this is how it must have happened. Jesus replied by telling them that this was an absurd assumption because this would mean that the kingdom of darkness was divided against itself and therefore could not stand! Jesus then said,

> "If I cast out demons by the Spirit of God, surely the Kingdom of God has come upon you. Or how can one enter a strong man's house and plunder his goods, unless he first binds the strong man? And then he will plunder his house." (Matt. 12:28–29)

To bind in rabbinical language is "to forbid" and *to loose* is "to permit." Jesus was simply making the point that He had bound. or forbidden, the demonic spirit from afflicting the man any longer and He had loosed the man from his infirmity. Please also note that this was on a horizontal level. By that, I mean that Jesus and the apostles when confronted by evil spirits or demons cast them out. They are never seen to be "binding principalities and powers by shouting into the heavens" (vertical).

The other passage in Matthew 18 also refers to things that can be bound and loosed. To literally translate the passage, it would read, "Whatever you loose on earth shall having been loosed in heaven" (Matt. 18:18). It does not read well when literally translated, but this basically means, the decisions the disciples were to make would be decisions that would agree with what heaven had already made. To understand this, we need to see the context of what is being said and not isolate verses and make them mean something else. The subject under discussion was when someone sins against another and how reconciliation should be sought and forgiveness granted. Keep this passage in mind:

> "Moreover if your brother sins against you, go and tell him his fault between you and him alone. If he

hears you, you have gained your brother." But if he will not hear you take with you one or two more, that by the mouth of two or more witnesses every word may be established. If he refuses to hear them, tell it to the church. But if he refuses even to hear the church, let him be to you a heathen and a tax collector. Assuredly I say to you whatever you bind on earth will be bound in heaven, and whatever you loose on earth will be loosed in heaven. Again I say to you if two of you agree on earth concerning anything they ask, it will be done for them by My Father in heaven. For where two or three are gathered together in My name, I am there in the midst of them." (Matt. 18:15–20)

The church has the power to bind and to loose—i.e., to forbid and to permit—in this context, to *forbid* the unrepentant, sinning brother fellowship with the church or to *permit* the repentant back into fellowship. When the church follows the teaching of Jesus and makes any decision along these lines, it is making a decision that is in line with what heaven has already decided.

One other scripture that should also be considered is found in Matthew 16:18–19:

I say to you that you are Peter and on this rock I will build My church and the gates of hell shall not prevail against it. And I will give you the keys of the kingdom of heaven, and whatever you bind on earth will be bound in heaven and whatever you loose on earth will be loosed in heaven.

The promise then is that the gates (strategies) of hell will not prevail or will not overcome the church and hell will not be able to resist the church that moves in the power and authority of the Lord. Jesus gives the keys (authority)—keys which have power to open and close, to give access or restrict. As we have seen in the other accounts where binding and loosing are mentioned, I believe this is again the power of the church to bring judgment into certain situations. And when the Gospel is preached and received, there is a *loosing* from the bondage of sin for the repentant and a *forbidding* (binding) on those who refuse.

To recap then, the early church never prayed binding prayers that were directed to principalities and powers in the heavens. Their prayers were directed to the Lord who always works on our behalf. The fervent prayer of a righteous man avails much. That is what James tells us, and that truth still stands. (Elijah was a man with a nature like ours, and he prayed earnestly that it would not rain and it did not rain on the land for three years and six months.)

Elijah prayed again and the heaven gave rain and the earth produced its fruit" (James 5:17–18). It is worthy of note that there are several key words in this scripture. Elijah didn't just pray and the heavens held back rain for three years and six months, but Elijah prayed fervently. The word *fervent* is also used to describe the fervent heat that will create a new heaven and a new earth in the future. This was no ordinary prayer—this was hot and passionate. Elijah meant business.

When God's people come together and they pray fervently, things happen, as they did in the prayer meeting in Acts 4. Hell shudders and shakes, and demons scramble when there is fervency in prayer. If only we could see the plight of lost souls and really understand the urgency of the hour, it would transform our prayer meetings!

The other thing to note is that it was not just a fervent prayer, but it came from a righteous man. Elijah's heart was in close fellowship with the Lord, so nothing restricted his prayers. No lurking sin obstructed his communication with heaven! We can also *bind* (forbid) the enemy in our own lives by not giving him any place.

Read what Scripture tells us:

> Therefore putting away lying, let each one of you
> speak truth with his neighbor, for we are members of

one another. Be angry and sin not, do not let the sun go down on your wrath, neither give place to the devil. Let him who stole steal no longer, but rather let him labor working with his hands what is good, that he may have something to give him who has need. Let no corrupt word proceed out of your mouth, but what is good for necessary edification, that it may impart grace to the hearers. And do not grieve the Holy Spirit of God, by whom you were sealed for the day of redemption. Let all bitterness, wrath anger clamor, and evil speaking be put away from you, with all malice. And be kind to one another tenderhearted, forgiving one another, even as God in Christ forgave you. (Eph. 4:25–32)

As we follow Paul's exhortation, the enemy is bound or forbidden. There are seasons and times that play their part in breaking through in hard places. Heaven will reveal one day the sacrifices that have been made, the prayers prayed, and the seed that has been sown by God's servants over the years, without some of them seeing the harvest but others have come at some later date and reaped what had been previously sown. One may sow, another may water, but it is God who gives the increase. Ultimately, He takes the glory because the Gospel, which is still the power of God unto salvation, is all about Him.

This is the Gospel we preach.

17

The Gospel That Proclaims
Christ's Second Coming

As already mentioned in a previous chapter, Paul was only in Thessalonica for three Sabbath days and yet a church was planted. This was a church commended by Paul for several reasons. The Bible says, "Remembering without ceasing your work of faith, labor of love, and patience of hope in our Lord Jesus Christ in the sight of our God and Father" (1 Thess. 1:3).

These believers had turned to God from their idols "to serve the living and true God and to wait for His Son from heaven whom He raised from the dead even Jesus who delivers from the wrath to come" (1 Thess. 1:9–10). Paul had obviously packed a lot of teaching into this short period of time and had taught them also of the promise of Christ's second coming.

In the next to the last verse in the New Testament, in Revelation 22:20, we are reminded again of Christ's coming: "Surely I am coming quickly."

There are well over three hundred references to the second coming of Christ in the New Testament, and twenty-three of the New Testament books mention His coming. Prophets spoke in the Old Testament of Christ's return and His kingdom upon earth.

Although this truth was a burning and purifying hope within the early church, it is often neglected in modern preaching. When this happens, it can produce Christians who are conformed to this world and squeezed into the mold of the present culture. Urgency for souls is lost, and carnal living can soon take the place of holiness. Of course, that is not always the case because each believer is responsible for their own lives and their own study of the scriptures, apart from what they may hear from the pulpit.

I remember some time ago teaching on the theme of the second coming of Christ, I searched through the modern songs and had difficulty finding any that related to this subject! Years ago, there were plenty of hymns written on this subject. As a young man recently saved, I would hear the congregation singing heartily,

> He's coming soon He's coming soon,
> With joy we welcome His returning,
> It may be morn, it may be night or noon,
> I know He's coming soon.

These were regular hymns and songs we sang, and looking back, I see the importance of biblical, doctrinal truths being sung. Many times, in our Gospel meetings, we would sing about the change Jesus Christ had made in our lives. These hymns would be an appeal in themselves for sinners to be saved. There was a time in South Wales years ago when the second coming was such a dominant part of the preaching that some people in the local church stopped mowing their lawns because they believed the coming of the Lord was so near! That obviously was an overreaction, but I share this to simply stress the point that the teaching of the nearness of Christ's return was a truth that was predominant in their preaching at that time.

When this is taught and believers catch this truth and really believe it, the effect is as the apostle John describes in 1 John 3:1–3:

> Behold what manner of love the Father has bestowed upon us that we should be called the children of God. Therefore the world does not know us, because it did

not know Him. Beloved now are we the children of God and it has not yet been revealed what we shall be, but we know that when He is revealed we shall be like Him for we shall see Him as He is. And everyone who has this hope in Him purifies himself, just as He is pure.

We cannot really believe this truth and live a carnal life! Purity of heart is the automatic outflow of the hope of His coming. One day, every believer will actually see Him and be like Him for we shall see Him as He is—the unchanging Christ, the man Christ Jesus, the one who will still bear the marks of Calvary in His body. When our earthly journey is over and all our trials are no more, to look upon His face will be reward enough for all our earthly labors. Another Gospel song comes to mind as I am writing is this:

> What a day that will be, when my Jesus I will see.
> When I look upon His face, the One who saved me
> by His grace,
> When He takes me by the hand, and leads me to the
> Promised Land,
> What a day glorious day that will be.

Allow me one more as these old hymns come flooding back!

> It will be worth it all, when we see Jesus,
> Life's trials will seem so small, when we see Christ,
> One glimpse of His dear face, all sorrow will erase,
> So bravely rune the race, till we see Christ.

When Jesus instituted what we call *communion*, or the *breaking of bread*, He told His disciples to do this in remembrance of Him until He comes again. The Lord never wanted the church to forget or to put this truth on the back burner, so to speak. In apostolic preaching, it was at the forefront; and it seems obvious from some scriptures that the early church were expecting His return soon. The Thessalonians had turned from idols to serve the Lord and wait for the return of Christ.

The disciples asked Jesus the all-important question, "What will be the sign of Your coming and of the end of the age?" (Matt. 24:3). It is important to remember that when Christ comes, it will not be the end of the world but the "end of the age." There will eventually be new heavens and a new earth, and righteousness will reign. We are living in an age of grace—an age where the longsuffering of God, as in the days of Noah, is very patient; where God, by the Holy Spirit and the preaching of the Gospel, is giving people the opportunity to repent and receive His salvation. As the disciples had asked this question concerning His return, He then answered them according to the questions they had posed. The disciples had been showing Jesus the buildings of the temple (Matt. 24:1). It was then that Jesus told them that there would not be one stone left upon another and that the temple would be destroyed.

This, of course, would be a shock to the disciples who were looking for the earthly kingdom of Christ to be set up. Instead, Jesus tells them of the destruction of the temple. They asked two questions, one in reference to the destruction of the temple and the other as to the sign of His coming and of the end of the age. The chapter must be interpreted in the light of these two questions which Jesus answers.

Among the signs, He mentions in this chapter are deception (v. 5); wars and rumors of wars (v. 6); famines, pestilences, and earthquakes (v. 7); persecution; (v. 9) many offended (v. 10); false prophets (v. 11); lawlessness (v. 12); and love of many growing cold (v. 12) There are also other signs relative to the coming of the Son of man such as the sun being darkened and the moon not giving its light, stars falling from heaven (v. 29). He also mentioned the sign of Noah's generation, which we will look at later.

Some interpret this chapter as to Jesus referring to signs regarding the destruction of the temple and that from Matthew 24:36, when Jesus speaks of the days of Noah, He was then speaking of signs that are relevant to the end of the age. I don't hold to this view because He had already spoken of His coming in Matthew 24:30–31, which tells us,

> Then the sign of the Son of Man will appear in heaven, and then all the tribes of the earth will mourn, and then they will see the Son of Man coming on the clouds of heaven with power and great glory, and He will send His angels with a great sound of a trumpet, and they will gather together His elect from one end of heaven to the other.

It would be true to say that many of the signs can be related to the destruction of the temple, which happened in AD 70, but there are others which cannot. To try and split the chapter into two distinct portions seems to be quite difficult. Other signs that have nothing to do with the destruction of the temple have yet to be fulfilled. The other observation is that while many of the signs would fit the destruction of the temple, they are also spoken of in some of the Epistles as being prevalent in the last days.

Read what 1 Timothy 4:1–3 says:

> Now the Spirit expressly says that in the latter times some will depart from the faith, giving heed to deceiving spirits and doctrines of demons, speaking lies in hypocrisy, having their own conscience seared with a hot iron, forbidding to marry and commanding to abstain from foods which God created to be received with thanksgiving by those who believe and know the truth.

Paul warns Timothy of the deception that will seek to infiltrate the church in the latter times. It is obvious from this scripture that the early church was looking for the coming of the Lord in their lifetime.

Also in Paul's second letter to Timothy, he writes of "perilous times" in the last days"

> But know this that in the last days perilous times will come; for men will be lovers of themselves, lovers of money, boasters, proud, blasphemers, disobedient to parents, unthankful, unholy, unloving, unforgiving, slanderers, without self-control, brutal despisers of good, traitors, headstrong, haughty, lovers of pleasure rather than lovers of God, having a form of godliness but denying its power. And from such turn away! (2 Tim. 3:1–5)

From these scriptures alone, we can conclude that the last days prior to the return of Christ, the world will not be a better place to live in—it will actually get worse!

In the light of these things, Paul charged Timothy to preach the Word and endure afflictions and do the work of an evangelist (2 Tim. 4:5). Darkness and light will clash even more in the last days, but "the Gospel is still the power of God unto salvation," as we read in Romans 1:16.

There will be those who have a form of godliness but deny the power of the Gospel. These will be people who are religious without any experience. One of the great problems in today's church is raising the level of awareness of God's people to His presence. Many are satisfied with much less than God intended us to experience. A few worship songs and a nice sermon with a happy fellowship time is all that many know and are satisfied with while the presence of God and His power are never really experienced. We need a fresh hunger again that will drive us to our knees and for the church to cry out again for the manifestations of His presence. A world that will be drowning in deception and self-gratitude where lawlessness abounds will need to see an alternative society of men and women who have an experience with God that can offer hope, faith, and life in the midst of the darkness.

Having mentioned these things, I still believe that the manifestations of God, the Holy Spirit, and power will also increase in the last days. I don't believe the church will be hanging on with its fingertips anxiously waiting for the Lord to come and deliver them from the mess the world is in but, rather, will be a church that is advancing the kingdom, reaching the nations, and experiencing latter-day outpourings and infillings of the Holy Spirit.

Having described a little of what the scriptures tell concerning the last days, let's go back to the book of Genesis and the account of Noah because Jesus said "As it was in the days of Noah." One thing is certain: in Noah's day, "the wickedness of man was great in the earth and every intention of the thoughts of his heart was only evil continually" (Gen. 6:5).

It was such wickedness that the Lord was sorry He had made man on the earth, and God was actually grieved in His heart (v. 6). This generation was so evil that God had to start again with just with one family—Noah's. The world perished in the flood!

However, when speaking of the days prior to His return, Jesus doesn't mention the gross evil of Noah's day but, rather, the total unconcern they had for the message and warning that Noah preached:

> For as in the days before the flood they were eating and drinking, marrying and giving in marriage, until the day that Noah entered the ark, and did not know until the flood came and took them all away, so also will the coming of the Son of Man be. (Matt. 24:38–39)

When I was in Bible college, we had a lecturer by the name of John Whitfield Foster. He had been a missionary to Israel and was there during the declaration of Israel becoming a nation again in 1948. Whenever the scripture came up in his teaching regarding "two shall be in the field one shall be taken and the other left and two women will be grinding at the mill; one shall be taken and the other left" (Matt. 24:40–41), he made it clear he believed this was not the rapture (the catching away of the church) but, rather, judgment coming upon unbelievers.

As students, we seemed to think this was referring to the rapture and always smiled and gave him a hard time, but the more I think about it, the more I think he was right. The context is that of judgment!

Noah's day presents us then with gross wickedness and total unconcern for God. It also is used to bring home the truth that when Jesus returns, there will be the element of surprise—that is, "they did not know until the flood came and took them all away" (Matt. 24:39). There will be signs that the believer must discern, but despite these, the unbelieving world will carry on as normal. There will be great wickedness but a belief that all things remain the same, so they will go about their lives as the Bible says "eating and drinking marrying and giving in marriage until!" (Matt. 24:38).

It will seem like any ordinary day, but it will be extraordinary. It will change everything. Paul describes it similar to a thief coming in the night:

> The day of the Lord so comes as a thief in the night. For when they will say "Peace and Safety!" then sudden destruction comes upon them, as labor pains upon a pregnant woman. And they shall not escape. But you brethren are not in darkness so that this day should overtake you as a thief. (1 Thess. 5:2–4).

The only announcement that will be given prior to His coming are the signs. Apart from these, He will come unannounced as a thief would come in the night.

Paul teaches of the judgment that will take place at His coming:

> When the Lord Jesus is revealed from heaven with His mighty angels, in flames of fire taking vengeance on those who do not know God, and on those who do not

obey the Gospel of our Lord Jesus Christ. These shall be punished with everlasting destruction from the presence of the Lord and from the glory of His power when he comes in that Day to be glorified in His saints and to be admired among all those who believe, because our testimony among you was believed. (2 Thess. 1:7–10)

In 2 Peter 3, Peter teaches that there will be those who will scoff at the thought of Christ's coming in the last days but reminds us that in the days of Noah, it was the longsuffering of God that waited because He was not willing that any should perish but all should come to repentance. Despite Noah's pleading and God's longsuffering, the world then refused to believe. Similarly, there will be those who scoff at such a thought and will continue on with their lives and their sin in the last days.

Peter also reminds that the Lord will come as a thief in the night and that the heavens will pass away with a great noise and the elements will melt with fervent heat and the earth will be burned up. There will be new heavens and a new earth in which righteousness dwells.

There are many other things that could be mentioned, but the most important is that Christ is coming back. He made that clear to His followers in John 14:3: "If I go to prepare a place for you, I will come again and receive you to Myself that where I am there you will be also."

As Jesus ascended from the Mount of Olives and the disciples stood gazing up into heaven as the cloud of glory received Him out of their sight, two angels announced, "This same Jesus who was taken up into heaven will so come in the same manner as you saw Him go into heaven" (Acts 1:9–11).

So far, we have looked at some of the signs of His coming and also as to the judgment upon unbelievers. But for the believer, the coming of Christ is a glorious hope, an event to look forward to and anticipate. I should make clear at this point that I do not see a secret catching away of the church, or rapture as it is called, with emphasis being placed on the word *secret*.

If Jesus is coming in flames of fire and with mighty angels, as Paul teaches, how can this be *secret*? I don't believe the world will wake up one day and suddenly find millions of people are missing, although movies have been made that depict this.

The context of Paul's teaching in 1 Thessalonians 4:13–17 is to do with assuring the believers regarding those who have already died in Christ that they will return with the Lord. This occasion will be marked with a shout with the voice of the archangel and with the trumpet of God and the dead will rise first and then believers will be caught up together with them to meet the Lord in the air.

If there is going to be a shout, this will be a shout that I can only imagine will be a thunderous shout that will cause the dead bodies of believers to rise from their graves. There will also be the trumpet of God. Trumpets were blown in the Old Testament for a number of reasons, one being to gather the troops for battle and also to call a special gathering of the people. So far, we have the shout of the archangel, the blast of the trumpet of God, and in 2 Thessalonians 1:8–9, we have mighty angels and the Lord Jesus Christ coming in flames of fire! There is no way this can be secret! The world will know what has taken place.

It is not my intention to try and fit all the pieces together relative to the second coming of Christ—i.e., the rapture, the tribulation, the millennial reign of Christ—I will leave that to those who are far better teachers than me on this subject. I simply want to make clear that the second coming of Christ was a central part of the apostles' message, and today everyone needs to be aware and ready for this great event.

One last thought on the subject of being ready is when Jesus told several parables to illustrate the importance of this, one being the parable of the ten virgins.

"Then shall the kingdom of heaven be likened unto ten virgins, which took their lamps, and went forth to meet the bridegroom. Now five of them were wise and five were foolish. Those who were foolish took their lamps and took no oil with them, but the wise took oil in their vessels with their lamps. While the bridegroom was delayed they all slumbered and slept. And at midnight there was a cry made, 'Behold the bridegroom is coming go out to meet Him!' Then all those virgins arose, and trimmed their lamps. And the foolish said unto the wise, 'Give us your oil; for our lamps are going out. But the wise answered, saying, 'No lest there should not be enough for us and you; but go and buy for yourselves.' And while they went to buy the bridegroom came, and those who were ready went in with him to the wedding and the door was shut. Afterward the other virgins came also saying, 'Lord, Lord open to us!' But he answered and said 'Assuredly, I say to you. I do not know you.' Watch therefore, for you know neither the day nor the hour in which the Son of Man is coming." (Matt. 25:1–13)

To understand the parable, we need to understand the custom of the day in Jesus's time.

Before a marriage, there was the engagement. This was a formal agreement between the two respective fathers. Following this, there was a betrothal; promises were made between the bridegroom and his fiancée in the presence of witnesses in the bride's parent's home. Presents were given by the bridegroom to his fiancée. It was after this that the bridegroom would go back to his father's house and build an addition onto his father's house for himself and his bride to occupy when finished. This addition to the house would have to be completed to his father's approval before the wedding could take place. This period of time could be about a year. When everything was ready, the bridegroom went along with his friends to call his bride to the marriage feast at his father's house.

It is probably this that Jesus was referring to in this parable. The shout in the streets could be heard "Behold the bridegroom is coming." The bridal party had to be ready at any time to go out to meet him.

Jesus made a promise to His disciples when He said,

"Let not your hearts be troubled; you believe in God believe also in Me. In My Father's house are many mansions [rooms] if it were not so I would have told you. I go to prepare a place for you and if I go and prepare a place for you, I will come again and receive you to Myself: that where I am, there you may be also." (John 14:1–3)

Jesus also said, "But of that day and hour no one knows, not even the angels of heaven, but My Father only" (Matt. 24:36).

The book of the Revelation tells us there will be a marriage supper of the Lamb, Jesus, and His bride: "Let us be glad and rejoice and give Him glory, for the marriage of the Lamb has come, and His wife has made herself ready" (Rev. 19:7).

In Ephesians 5, in Paul's teaching on the relationship between husbands and wives, he relates this to the great mystery of Christ and His church. And in Ephesians 5:25, we find this wonderful verse: "Husbands love your wives just as Christ loved the church and gave Himself for her."

Every born-again believer will one day be part of the great marriage supper of the Lamb of God who gave Himself for us when He died on Calvary's cross. And one day, He will return for His bride. Are you ready? Do you know Him? He's coming!

This is the Gospel we preach.

18

The Gospel and Discipleship

Just before Jesus ascended to His Father, His disciples were assembled with Him on the Mount of Olives; and He gave them what is called the Great Commission. We read this in Matthew 28:18–20:

> "All authority has been given to Me in heaven and on earth. Go therefore and make disciples of all nations, baptizing them in the name of the Father and of the Son and of the Holy Spirit, teaching them to observe all things that I have commanded you and lo I am with you always to the end of the age."

The Gospel message calls people out of sin and spiritual darkness—it convicts; demands repentance; and leads to forgiveness, salvation, and life. People are born again of the Holy Spirit; and as Peter exhorts, he calls the new believers spiritual newborn babes who he encouraged to desire the pure milk of the Word that they may grow in their faith (1 Pet. 2:2). Notice how he addresses them as "newborn babes." If all we do is preach the Gospel and bring people to new birth, we miss the whole point of the Great Commission. It was actually to make disciples, not just new converts.

Babies need attention. They need a lot of love and care, they have to be taught and trained in the way to behave, and they need milk and eventually solid foods. One thing is for sure: if you leave the baby unattended, there will be problems! The same things happen very often when newborn babes in Christ are not disciplined.

I could say it's easy to disciple new believers if they want to be disciples! I can't think why someone would not want to be if they have truly come to know the Lord Jesus Christ, but sometimes it is a struggle to have them make time in what seems to be so often busy schedules. Having said that, people generally make time for what they regard as really important.

I remember driving through a busy seaside resort in England one evening. The weather was lashing down rain, and my wife Val and I could see the waves pounding the promenade wall. There was no one walking on the promenade. The strong wind and rain had kept most people in doors, except for one man! We could hardly believe our eyes as we drove by this solitary individual who stood facing the swelling waves. He was fishing!

The moral of the story is, if people really want to do something, they will so often find a way to do it. What a great illustration of commitment to fishing! His dedication was simply born out of his love for fishing. When people fall in love with Jesus, dedication to Him automatically follows; and when it does, it makes disciplining easy.

Too often we have people who easily make a decision for Christ but don't really want to follow Him. Sometimes we are left wondering what went wrong and why there seems to be no desire for the things of God. Perhaps the answer is that some have made just a mental ascent to the truth and there has been no supernatural new birth.

There are many things that come into play that hinder people from making themselves available to become a disciple. We should also note that we are dealing with a culture very often that demands so much of their time and energy that even getting people to a small group in a home is a battle. I remember Bill Hybels saying at one of the Willow Creek conferences, "Our competition is not the church down the road but everything that competes for people's time out in the world." I notice a vast difference between the cultures around the world and the willingness to be available for discipleship.

Having said that we should not make that an excuse and give up otherwise we are bound to fail.

The other important thing to remember is that disciples are not *born*, they are *made*. "Go and *make* disciples" is said in Scripture. They have to be made, and we are the ones who have to do it! They don't just appear one day in church as a ready-made disciple; they come newly born again but with so many things in their lives that are still clinging on to them from their old life before conversion.

Lazarus was raised from the dead, but when he appeared outside the tomb, he still had the grave clothes wrapped around him. Jesus said "Loose him and let him go" (John 11:44). There are the old habits that need to be broken; the lusts of the old nature that need to crucified; guilt, shame, and fears that they have lived with for so long; financial problems and marriage problems; and more. The person may have been born again, but how to follow Christ and to get rid of the grave clothes is another matter and that is where discipleship is needed.

When Jesus was ministering, large crowds followed Him and amazing miracles occurred; but the interesting thing is that in the upper room, waiting for the outpouring of the Holy Spirit, there were just one hundred and twenty followers. Jesus was more interested in making disciples than simply gathering large crowds. He wasn't leaving a megachurch behind, just relatively few disciples that He would trust to take this Gospel to the then-known world. It was with the twelve Jesus spent most of His time, although on one occasion He had sent seventy out to spread the message. At the end, it was the twelve and the three who were closest to Him—Peter, James, and John. So the question we must ask is *How did Jesus disciple these men?* and *What were some of the key principles He used?*

To understand the background of Jewish life in Jesus's day, it was the hope of many of the young men in Israel that one day they may be so well versed and learned in the scriptures and the law that they would have the opportunity to follow a rabbi. To be a follower meant that you would walk in his footsteps, so to speak. You would ask questions and be completely submitted to learn from Him, from his teachings, and from his way of life.

It wasn't easy to be chosen to follow a rabbi. Often, it was the student who would ask the rabbi if he could become a follower; but it was only the most promising students that would be given that opportunity. To the rest, the rabbi would probably tell them to go home and work in their family business, marry have a family, and become a good citizen in their community. It is most probable that Peter and Andrew along with James and John had not reached the standard of knowledge in the law and scriptures and had returned to their hometown and business. But then, one day, Jesus, the greatest rabbi of all, walked by and said, "Come follow Me, and I will make you fishers of men" (Mark 1:17).

They recognized Him as a rabbi (teacher), as did the Sadducees (Matthew 22:24), a rich man (Matt. 19:16), a lawyer (Matt. 22:36), and so did the Pharisees (Luke 19:39). These fishermen Jesus called that day hadn't made the grade and probably had felt disappointed and failures. The wonderful thing about Jesus is that He calls failures to become disciples!

They left their nets as this was the opportunity of a lifetime. They were now going to walk in the dust of the feet of the greatest rabbi of all. They didn't realize it at that moment, but they were in for the time of their life—three and a half years of walking with Him, learning of and from Him, and seeing miracle after miracle. It would be a roller coaster. There would be great exhilaration as they witnessed miracles beyond their wildest dreams, heartbreak when they witnessed the cross, and followed by unbelievable joy when He rose from the dead!

Now Jesus has to start work making these fishermen into disciples who eventually would risk everything for Him.

Relationship Is Vital

This wasn't going to be simply teacher and student; this was going to be relational—the Master befriending them, drawing them alongside, and sharing the secrets of the Kingdom with them. Disciples are not made without relationship!

Matthew 4 records all kinds of sickness and diseases healed shortly after calling these fishermen. Many demon-possessed victims were delivered, epileptics, paralytics, and great crowds followed Him. But then we find Matthew 5. Jesus goes up on a mountain with His disciples and begins to teach them. These were His priority, not the crowds who had come for miracles, but the ones who wanted to become followers. He was now going to invest His time into these men who one day would turn the world upside down. Too often we are interested in crowds, and we make that our priority.

Every preacher wants to preach to a crowd rather than a few, but we also have to recognize that it is the disciples we make that will multiply our ministry. It is the disciples who will go on to plant new churches, and it is by making disciples that the work of the Kingdom will grow in spiritual health and so will the local church that we may be involved with. It is the disciples who stand when the storms of life are fierce, when the valley is dark and long. It is the disciples who will walk out of that valley changed, knowing God in a deeper, more intimate way and will show by their life and walk with the Lord that the Kingdom of God is real and the King is worth following.

It was on this mount that Jesus taught them what we call the beatitudes: "Blessed are the pure in spirit, those who mourn, the meek, those who hunger and thirst for righteousness, the merciful, the pure in heart, the peacemakers, those who are persecuted" (Matt. 5). He didn't give them a lecture on signs and wonders immediately after all the excitement of the miracles but chose to talk to them about character principles.

It is interesting that when the apostle Paul lists the qualifications for elders and deacons in 1 Timothy 3 and Titus 1, the emphasis is also on *character*, not charisma. Jesus sat down and taught them—unhurried with time for questions—the Master and His students were relating as He unfolded eternal truths. They were now soaking in truths that set free, that liberate the soul, and that they were to recall time and again in the future when the pressure was on and persecution was rife. What a privilege it was to sit at His feet and learn from Him and also, as the days passed by, to become more at ease in their relationship with Him. The person who is "discipling" must always make sure a relationship is being fostered, not because it is the right thing to do but because of genuine love and concern that the new believer will reach the destiny God has called them to.

Jesus was always interested in relationships; He was even called a friend of sinners! He went to Peter's house and saw his wife's mother sick with a fever, and as the Bible says, "He touched her hand and the fever left her" (Matt. 8:14–15). He taught His disciples (Luke 10) to look for the man of peace (one who is receptive to their message) and, when finding that person, to stay with him speak to the family and heal the sick in the household. It is far better for the whole household to be saved and following Jesus than for the household to be divided. Jesus loved relating to people. When He called Matthew to follow Him, Matthew threw a party for his friends and Jesus was invited, which we read in Luke 5:29: "Then Levi [Matthew] gave Him a great feast in his own house and there were a number of tax collectors and sinners with them."

What a great idea Matthew had when he invited a number of his friends to the party to share with them that he was going to become a follower and disciple of Jesus. One of the greatest tools we have for evangelism is our homes and food! What appears to be a social event can become a turning point in people's lives.

The interesting thing is that Jesus was pleased to accept the invitation, just as He was to attend the wedding in Cana of Galilee. He was happy to be among people to answer their questions to relate to them on a social level. When things like this happen within the home, they affect family members. We miss so many great opportunities if our homes become our castles rather than places where evangelism and discipleship can take place.

Too often the Christian church has simply invited strangers to a strange building (church) to hear someone who, to them, is a stranger and we wonder why things don't work! Churches that grow are where the people are building relationships with unbelievers and recognize that very often, through those relationships, the unbeliever sees the Christian life modeled before they ever darken the door of a church.

When they eventually do accept an invitation to attend a church service, they are not surprised by the style of worship or the prayer ministry for the sick. They have already been advised certain things may happen in the service and the reason why those things may be different from a traditional church service. Relationship is important with the unbeliever and must continue with the new believer if we are to see people come to Christ and then become disciples. Jesus invited Himself to the home of Zachius the tax collector, and as a result the whole family received salvation. It all happened in a home!

The believers in the book of Acts continually met in each other's homes as we learn in Acts 2:46: "So continuing daily with one accord in the temple and breaking bread from house to house they ate their food with gladness and simplicity of heart."

It was in homes where they not only learned the apostle's doctrine, prayed together, and broke bread together; but they ate and fellowshipped together. It would be in these times where discipleship would take place with the new believers together. It would be in that kind of setting that new believers would hear the truths of the Kingdom of God and be encouraged to become fully devoted followers of Jesus Christ.

In those times of fellowship, close relationships would be formed and the process of discipleship would continue to grow. This became the DNA of the early church. It was Barnabus who befriended Paul after his conversion when the other apostles were hesitant to believe he truly was a follower of Christ (Acts 9:27).

Paul discovered around twelve disciples of John the Baptist in the city of Ephesus. He was the one who shared with them what John's message of the coming Christ was really all about, and he prayed for them to receive the Holy Spirit and then they were baptized in water. Paul discipled these new believers who were to eventually see an amazing revival (Acts 19). It was in Paul's confinement under the Romans in Acts 28:23–31 that he continued to teach and preach the Gospel and disciple new believers. Keep in mind these passages:

> Many came to him at his lodging, to whom he explained and solemnly testified of the kingdom of God, persuading them concerning Jesus from both the law of Moses and the Prophets, from morning till evening. (Acts 28:23)
>
> Then Paul spent two whole years in his own rented house, and received all who came to him, preaching the kingdom of God and teaching the things which concern the Lord Jesus Christ with all confidence, no one forbidding him. (Acts 28:30–31)

Paul was a leader, and he inspired people. Remember, in all our relationships in the process of discipling others, in order for the relationship to lead to change in the new believer's life, they must be inspired by our lifestyle.

Modeling Life

Paul could say "Imitate me even as I imitate Christ" (1 Cor. 11:1). To bring the new believer into the fullness of the life of Christ and see discipleship principles worked through in his or her life, we have to model that life. We have to be moving in the right direction for the new believer to follow us. Paul was constantly seeking to press forward into a greater knowledge of Christ (Phil. 3:13). To be a member of Paul's team or to have him as a spiritual father would be a constant challenge to one's Christian life and experience. When saying farewell to the elders of the church at Ephesus as we read in Acts 20:17–38, he spoke about his manner of life that he had lived among them:

> What manner I have always lived among you, serving the Lord with all humility, with many tears and trials which happened to me by the plotting of the Jews. (Acts 20:18–19)

He had modeled the life of Jesus who also served with humility. Jesus was the one who made Himself of no reputation when He came to this earth and humbled Himself even to the death of the cross (Phil. 2). The elders at Ephesus had been privileged to work with an apostle who followed the great apostle and author of our faith, Jesus.

Imagine the effect that had upon these men whom Paul had discipled. Pride had no place in Paul's heart because he reminded himself of what he was by the grace of God: "But by the grace of God I am what I am, and His grace toward me was not in vain, but I labored more abundantly than they all yet not I, but the grace of God which was with me" (1 Cor. 15:10).

It was Jesus who wept on a number of occasions as recorded in scripture, but apart from the ones recorded, there would be many more times, when He was all alone praying to His Father, that tears would course down His cheeks as He contemplated the devastation sin had wrought upon humanity. Paul would have taught these elders the important principle of humility and would have gathered around him men who followed his manner of life.

Paul declared to them, "I kept back nothing that was helpful but proclaimed it to you and taught you publicly and from house to house" (Acts 20:20).

During those times, as they met in homes, they would eat together, forge close relationships, ask questions, and drink in the truth as the inspiration and vision of the apostle rubbed off on them. Despite all the trials Paul went through, he exhibited a great sense of joy in serving the Lord; and although bonds and afflictions were prophesied if he went to Jerusalem, this did not deter the apostle from pressing on to what he believed to be the will of God and neither did he allow these things to steal his joy (Acts 20:23–24).

Paul also was in no way interested in making money from his ministry but in simply declaring the Gospel and making disciples! This we learn in this scripture:

> I have coveted no one's silver or gold apparel. Yes, you yourselves know that these hands have provided for my necessities and for those who were with me. I have shown you in every way by laboring like this that you must support the weak. And remember the words of the Lord Jesus, that He said, "It is more blessed to give than to receive." (Acts 20:33–35)

These elders had a great love for Paul which was shown by the fact that they wept freely on Paul's neck and kissed him (Acts 20:37). Again, we see here that these men had not been educated in a classroom as students with teacher, but they had been discipled by Paul's manner of life through friendship and relationship.

Timothy looked up to Paul as a spiritual father, and Paul called him a true son in the faith (2 Tim. 1:2). In mentoring and discipling the young pastor Timothy, in the opening verse of 1 Timothy 1:1, Paul makes it clear that the call to the ministry was by the commandment of God and the Lord Jesus Christ and was in no way through man's own efforts or striving. Paul wasn't an apostle by his own choice but by God's. The young pastor Timothy would recognize that Paul was completely submitted to the will of God. To follow this man, there was no half measures! The principle of producing after our kind holds fast also when discipling others.

Prayer

Jesus showed His disciples the importance of prayer by living a lifestyle of prayer. They were affected to such a degree that they asked Him to teach them to pray. The disciples witnessed firsthand what it meant to really intercede:

> In the days of His flesh when He had offered up prayers and supplications, with vehement cries and tears to Him who was able to save Him from death, and was heard because of His godly fear. (Heb. 5:7)

Matthew records His prayer in the garden of Gethsemane just prior to His arrest and eventual crucifixion (Matt. 26:38–46). With sweat drops like blood falling from His brow, Jesus prayed to the Father. Obedience to the will of God was greater than the suffering that was soon to follow; and while He could be heard with His loud cries and pleadings with the Father, the disciples not only recognized what real intercession was, but they also saw complete surrender and submission to the will of God.

They would never forget that moment and what was to follow shortly after. In their own trials and tribulations that would accompany them later as they spread the Gospel, they too would turn to prayer and no doubt there were many times when tears and loud cries would be their own experience. They would know what to do in the hour of trial because they had seen it modeled by Jesus Himself.

To spend some time actually praying with the person who is being discipled is very important. They need to hear and see the passion of prayer being lived out by the one who is discipling them. Short times of prayer that keeps the new believer fresh and inspired are better than long, protracted ones, which can leave him or her feeling like they are climbing a very steep hill and wondering if they will ever make it to the top!

Praying the Word of God and its promises and teaching the disciple to take hold of scripture and confess it, praying it over their own lives and that of their family, are a good place to start. Knowing the acceptance and righteousness of God as explained earlier in this book is all important for the foundation of faith and prayer. There are so many aspects of prayer, which is a subject all of its own, but the most important thing is to get the new believer to learn to relate to God in prayer and to sense His presence.

Questions

One of the things that any rabbi would do was to teach his disciples to ask questions. Sometimes, when asked a question, the rabbi would also pose another question. The great Rabbi Jesus, was just the same. This is one occasion as recorded in Matthew 21:23–32:

> Now when he came into the temple, the chief priests and the elders of the people confronted Him as he was teaching and said," By what authority are you doing these things? And who gave You this authority?" But Jesus answered and said to them, "I also will ask you one thing, which if you tell Me, I likewise will tell you by what authority I do these things: "The baptism of John where was it from? From heaven or from men?" And they reasoned among themselves, saying, "If we say from heaven, He will say to us, 'Why then did you not believe him?' But if we say, 'From men,' we fear the multitude, for all count John as a prophet."

They answered that they didn't know, so Jesus refused to tell them by what authority He did those things. He went on to tell them that, because they did not believe John but tax collectors and harlots did, they would enter the kingdom of God before them! What

Jesus said to them that day wasn't what they wanted to hear, and they probably wished they had never asked! But rabbis would often pose a question when asked one. If you notice also, when Jesus told parables, He didn't always make the parable crystal-clear even to His disciples. He knew, if they wanted to know the meaning and truth behind it, they would come and ask.

The parable of the sower recorded in Mark 5:3–20 is one example where the disciples and others around Him came and asked what it meant. Everything cannot just be put on a plate for the one who is being discipled; he or she must learn to search for answers and ask questions. Self-study is very good; in fact, we learn more when we research ourselves. Jesus wanted to see if the people were hungry for truth. When a person is hungry, they will seek food. If a person is really wanting to follow the great rabbi, they will ask questions and be eager to learn.

Self-study material can be given for the new believer to learn to search the scriptures, and times to meet with the teacher can be times when those things studied can be talked over and, if necessary further, explained. I wrote some years ago a little book entitled *New Life in Christ*. It is a ten-week study book which, for five days each week, gives scriptures to read along with some exposition and questions to answer. It is designed for the disciple and teacher to meet each week and be able to discuss what has been learned, or it can be used in a small group setting with a number of new believers.

It covers topics such as understanding new life, assurance, the new birth, water baptism, the Kingdom of God, and the local church and how it operates. Also, topics on prayer, strongholds, giving, the baptism of the Holy Spirit, and the gifts of the Spirit are discussed extensively. By taking the new believer through the basics of faith and helping him or her to understand these things, it provides a foundation on which they can build and start to grow spiritually. When this is done one to one or in a small group, questions can be asked and understanding gained.

A little boy asked his dad a question one day, "Dad, who won the heavyweight boxing championship in 1986?" His dad replied, "I don't know, son."

The boy asked another question "What is the longest river in the world, Dad?"

"I don't know son," his dad replied.

After asking another couple of questions and the same reply, "I don't know son," the little boy looked up at his dad and asked, "You don't mind me asking questions, do you, Dad?" to which his dad replied, "No, son, if you never ask, you never learn!"

New believers will ask questions; and if we don't know all the answers, we can always do some research ourselves and give them the answer later. When children reach the age where they can talk they are normally full of questions. One little girl was constantly asking the question *why*. Her mother got so fed up with hearing the word *why* that she said, "Will you just give that word a rest for a while?" To which the little girl replied "OK." But is it all right if I just say "How come?"

The fact is, they are trying to figure out the world they have been born into and so we get bombarded with questions. The new believer, having recently been born again into another kingdom— the Kingdom of God—should be encouraged to ask as many questions as they like. It's all part of the discipleship process and spiritual growth.

Opportunities for Hands-On Service

I am not the best at knowing what to do on a computer; in fact, I am typing this whole book with just two fingers! Sometimes I get on a roll and use three but then have to go back and delete a spelling mistake! My son, Mark, who works with me as associate pastor often gets a call from me to come into my office and show me how to attach documents and other computer-related problems.

The only problem is that he will come supposedly to show me how to do it, and he's done it himself before I can blink an eye! He will often say "Dad, do you not remember what I did last time?" I have to remind him that I basically paid for his college education when he was studying business and computers! But basically, I learn when I get to do it, not just watching him do it! Although even if I forget after that, I've learned I can now go on YouTube and watch a video of how to do it!

Learning how to do things is great, but actually doing them is very important. Jesus would use this principle when making disciples. They would watch Him heal the sick and cast out demons; but in His school of discipleship, they would then be sent out to do the same. There was an occasion when seventy disciples came back rejoicing because even demons were subject to them (Luke 10:1–20). They were told to heal the sick and look for the man of peace (as explained in an earlier chapter). Jesus brought them back to the most important thing to rejoice in—that is, their names were written in heaven. We read this in Luke 10:19–20:

> Behold I give you the authority to trample on serpents and scorpions, and over all the power of the enemy, and nothing shall by any means hurt you. Nevertheless do not rejoice in this, that the spirits are subject to you, but rather rejoice because your names are written in heaven.

The disciples were excited because they had hands-on experience. They had stepped up to another level in which they had been trusted to go and do what they had seen Jesus doing.

In every aspect of training, the time must come when the one being trained gets to do it themselves. We cannot train successfully without this principle. When praying for the sick, the discipler should have his disciple alongside also laying hands on the sick person, watching what happens in every situation. But then, there must come a time when the discipler stands back and says, "Now you do it."

Preachers, upcoming musicians, and worship leaders have to be given opportunities to preach and to take the lead. Opportunities for hands-on service are the times when we learn the most. Personal evangelism courses are great, but taking someone out on the streets or coffee bars and letting them start up conversations with nonbelievers is when they learn firsthand and have the opportunity to share their personal story. It may sound strange, but believers do need help at sharing their own story so that they don't use "churchy" words and theological words that the nonbeliever does not understand.

We should be able to share our story within just a few minutes—basically, telling of what we were like before conversion, how we came to Christ, and what changes in our lives that Jesus has made. These may be three simple parts to the story and, if given within just a few minutes, can have life-changing effects. The sad thing is that many who have attended church and have been believers over the years, unless they have been discipled, have little or no idea how to actually share their story with an unbeliever.

They do not know how to lead someone to the Lord; and as a result, they become believers who very rarely share anything of the Gospel to nonbelievers. This was never the DNA of the early church because they filled Jerusalem with their doctrine. A great book to read on this particular subject is a book called *T4T* by Steve Smith and Ying Kai. In Asia, by training and discipleship, within ten years, 1,738,143 water baptisms were recorded and 158,993 churches planted.

Many times, churches spend their time praying for *breakthroughs* when what is needed is a *breakout* of believers who have settled for nice meetings and a comfortable lifestyle.

I remember coming home for the summer break from Bible college as a young man and I felt the Lord challenge me to knock on every door in the village where I grew up. The thought of it made me nervous because everyone knew me; after all, it was just a small coal-mining village. I prayed and asked the Lord for courage and went to every door. When I had completed the task, I felt a sense of victory in my own spirit because I had not allowed fear to master me, and I had given everyone the opportunity to hear the Gospel.

Storms, Critics, and Atmosphere

The disciples watched Jesus handle the storm when the tempest threatened to capsize the boat they were in (Mark 4:39). They saw Him use an authority they had never witnessed before when He simply rebuked the storm and said "Peace be still." To rebuke it meant that it was satanically inspired. They learned a number of things that day that behind some of the things that appear to be natural, these things can be the schemes of the devil to keep them from reaching their destination. We have all had storms, I'm sure, that have attempted to keep us from our destiny and calling. Sometimes they seem to come out of nowhere when actually they come from hell itself! There are times when we also have to rise up in the authority that has been given to us and speak to the storm.

Jesus had His critics wherever He went. The Pharisees were always dogging His heels and generally part of the crowd, trying to catch Him out in His words. They thought they had the perfect opportunity when they threw the woman caught in the act of adultery at His feet and asked Him what should be done with her because Moses had commanded in the law that she should be stoned to death. But they failed as Jesus confronted them with their own sins.

They were always keen to criticize Him, but Jesus didn't allow any of those things to deter Him from doing the Father's will. The apostle Paul who modeled himself on Christ was just the same. As a prisoner awaiting execution, he was ready to be offered up to the One who had called him and could testify to having fought a good fight of faith. All great leaders have had their critics but have also learned that, when they are sure of their course in life, no criticism must be allowed to take them off course!

Jesus could not do many mighty miracles in Nazareth because of their unbelief, and all he did was heal a few sick people. When Jesus answered the request to go to the house of Jairus, whose daughter was sick, He arrived only to find the girl had died and the mourners were gathered. When He told them that she was only sleeping, they laughed and mocked Him.

Before Jesus raised her from the dead, He had the same people who had mocked Him removed from the house. It was all to do with atmosphere! The disciples would begin to learn the importance of the atmosphere of the presence of the Father and the things that hinder His presence. This was all part of their training as one day they would be relying on the Holy Spirit to take them to the then known world with the Gospel message. For miracles to occur, there must be the atmosphere of faith; unbelief hinders the supernatural flow of the Holy Spirit.

Every day, they were learning something new as they walked alongside the great Rabbi Jesus. This journey would take them to the ultimate sacrifice when they would see Him offered up on the cross; and in the midst of suffering that no words can describe, He looked down at His mother Mary and said to His mother, "Woman, behold your son." As His eyes then looked toward His disciple, John, He said, "Behold your mother." This was the ultimate trust that He placed in John.

There comes a time when disciples have to take hold of the baton, remembering all they have learned and run with the vision and message that God has entrusted them with. This is exactly what happened just prior to Jesus's ascension as He commissioned them to take the Gospel to the ends of the earth. He was basically saying, "I am trusting you with the evangelization of the world. When you are filled with the Holy Spirit. then you must go and make disciples." He had trained them and made them disciples, and He then handed the baton to them we call the Great Commission. When the Holy Spirit was poured out upon them, the DNA of world evangelism and discipleship became part of them. The world was waiting to be turned upside down!

This is the Gospel we preach.

19

The Great Commission
and the Promise

When Jesus gave His disciples the Great Commission to go and make disciples of all nations, He also gave them a wonderful promise recorded in Matthew 28:20: "I am with you always even to the end of the age."

As they went with the good news of the Gospel, they knew they were not alone when they preached the message both in Jerusalem, Judea, Samaria, and to the outermost parts of the world. The Christ of the cross and the empty tomb promised to be with them in power and with all the authority that had been given to Him in heaven and on earth.

Last-minute instructions had been given to Jesus's followers as He stood with them on the Mount of Olives just prior to His ascension back to heaven. Although He would no longer be visible to their natural eyes, He promised He would still be with them. Despite all the battles that lay ahead, the persecution, trials, and hardships they would face, He would be there standing with them.

We don't have to look too far in the book of Acts to read the account of Stephen's martyrdom; yet as he was being stoned, he saw a vision of the Son of man standing on the right hand of the Father in heaven. What happened had not gone unnoticed by heaven.

When writing to Timothy in his second letter, the apostle Paul tells of his soon departure from this world as recorded in 2 Timothy 4:6: "I am already being poured out as a drink offering, and the time of my departure is at hand, I have fought a good fight, I have finished the race, I have kept the faith.

Paul knew his execution was not too far away as he remained a prisoner under Roman arrest. In his first defense, no one had stood with him and he writes that all had forsaken him (2 Tim. 4:16). However, the next verses are all important:

> But the Lord stood with me and strengthened me, so that the message might be preached fully through me, and that all the Gentiles might hear. Also I was delivered out of the mouth of the Lion. And the Lord will deliver me from every evil work and preserve me for His heavenly kingdom. To Him be glory for ever and ever. Amen! (2 Tim. 4:17–18)

The Lord Jesus was true to His promise; and even when others had forsaken the apostle, He didn't. Not only did Jesus stand with Paul in his hour of need, but He strengthened him, in order for Paul to continue to preach the Gospel.

While the world rushes headlong into sin, God looks down and sees lost souls in every tribe and nation, from the mansions of Hollywood and the multimillion dollar homes of the wealthy to the little mud huts in the villages of Africa. There are needy souls who must have an opportunity to hear the Gospel. We, who have had the privilege of hearing and responding to the offer of salvation through Jesus Christ, owe it to the world around us to share the good news.

Some may never make it to the outermost parts of the world; but our world starts in our home, our neighborhoods, our towns, and our cities. You may never walk through the airport to board an airplane to some remote part of the world, but are you willing to walk across the road to speak to your neighbor? Are you willing to walk up to that person in the shopping mall as the Holy Spirit prompts you? Or are you willing to sit down with relatives and share the story of your conversion?

One of the greatest blessings as my wife Val and I have ministered in conferences around the world has been to see young men and women respond to the call of God to the ministry. In recent trips to Uganda, Namibia, and Madagascar, it was amazing to see young people fill the front of the church in response to the call of God upon their lives to the ministry. I often wonder what God will do with them in the future. We always encourage each one to talk to their pastors and ask what the next step to preparing for future ministry will be.

There may be those whom God will use to shake the continent of Africa in the future or who will do some mighty work for the Lord wherever He may send them. One day, heaven will reveal everything that has taken place; and we will be in for some wonderful surprises, I'm sure.

From those early days of the birth of the church until this present time, this Gospel has been preached. Some have paid the ultimate price of laying down their lives; others have labored in foreign lands at great sacrifice. Some died young, others lived to old age, and some struggled with sickness but still preached the Gospel. Some have been used of God to pastor megachurches and others have been faithful in smaller church congregations. Some are well known and others are unknown. But the Lord knows each one; and whatever our calling and wherever God sends us, the Lord promises to be with us!

It was with little trepidation that several years ago Val and I were invited to go to a remote village called Kapyani in Uganda. Our friend Kephous Ndinywa and his wife, Rebecca, drove us to this village several hours' travel time from Kampala where Kephous's younger brother Fred is pastor of the village church. Kephous grew up in the village, his older brother Samuel being the first in the family to become a Christian. Samuel was basically disowned and asked to leave the village when he became a Christian; but through his prayers and witness, eventually, the whole family was saved.

As we left the main road on our way to the village, we encountered miles upon miles of dirt roads with huge bumps and potholes. We have been told that you have to have a PhD in driving in Uganda, which basically means "pothole driver"! The other funny story we were told is that anyone driving in a straight line in Uganda must be drunk!

As we traveled along the dirt roads, Kephous encouraged us by saying, "I am taking you to the ends of the earth." Of course, I had read that phrase in the Bible, but every bump and pothole we encountered reminded me this was a reality! We spent several days ministering to these lovely people and noticed, while we were there, that they had no clean drinking water. Never in the history of that little village had they had any clean drinking water. Kephous would tell us that it is a miracle that he and his family had survived.

There was a hole in the ground; and when the bucket was pulled up, it was full of dirty water that I would not have let my dog drink! We knew we had to do something to raise money for a well to be bored. My wife, Val, went over to the UK and preached in several churches, and most of the money was raised in just a short time. Other individuals gave, and we were able to give the go-ahead for a company to bore a well in that village. The well now provides them with crystal-clear drinking water for which we are grateful to all the churches and individuals who have given money to make this possible.

To return to the story of Kephous's brother Samuel, although basically disowned, he returned on a number of occasions to the village. On one of these visits, he told them that he had received a vision from the Lord that there would be a well bored in the village and pointed to the exact spot where it would be. This was too much for his father to comprehend, and Samuel was looked upon as though this religion had affected his brain!

It was several years later when we were ministering in the village that I was told this story by Samuel. He said the well-boring company came and did tests to ascertain the best place to bore for water. The very place where the well was bored was the exact spot he had seen in his vision! Praise the Lord for His goodness!

We have raised money for medical doctors to spend time in the village on one of our visits, and they were able to give medications and prescriptions to one thousand people in four days. At the time of writing, the village has just had an agricultural tractor delivered for which, again, churches and individuals raised money. This will enable them to plow the land and help the whole village with fresh produce. I am told they have two harvests per year, the weather is good, and so is the soil.

Despite all the poverty and needs of the village, Pastor Fred and his team have planted another fourteen churches from the mother church in Kapyani. These things never make the popular Christian magazines, but they have heaven's attention. These people—like countless millions around the world—have proved, when you preach this Gospel, lives are changed, souls saved, churches planted, and through all the tests trials and hardships, the Lord Himself stands with them.

He is always true to His word, always keeps His promises. He is the central figure and the One who paid the ultimate sacrifice for our sins.

If you have never met Him and received Him as your Savior, now is the time to do it. Call upon Him, repent of the sin and unbelief that has kept you blinded to the Gospel of Good News and salvation, and as you pray, believe the Word of God, which promises "Whoever shall call upon the name of the Lord shall be saved" (Rom. 10:13).

If you are a preacher of the Gospel, believe the promise that the Lord Jesus will be with you even to the ends of the earth wherever your ministry takes you. Whatever your calling and wherever you are laboring for Him, whether it be on some mission field of the world or in a local church, remember, the Lord is with you.

He is the same Lord who spoke to Moses from the burning bush and declared Himself to be "I AM WHO I AM" (Exod. 3:13). He is the One who is unchanging and always the same, who stood alongside Moses as he stood before the great pharaoh. He was the One who was with Joseph even when he was in prison in fetters of iron (Ps. 105:13).

He was with Daniel in the lions' den and with Shadrach Meshach and Abed-Nego in the fiery furnace (Dan. 3:20, 6:22). He stood alongside His prophets as they declared the Word of the Lord. He stood alongside Paul in shipwreck and imprisonment and many tribulations (2 Cor. 11:23–28). He has always stood alongside His servants down the centuries as they have taken this Gospel to the ends of the earth. His promise still holds fast in this generation. He still declares to every one of us who know Him as Savior, "I will never leave you or forsake you" (Heb. 13:5).

I remind you again of the great promise Jesus made to His disciples: "I am with you even to the end of the age."

One of the most touching things that was said to Val and I as we met the pastors and their wives in the village of Kapyani for the first time was, "We know God must love us, because He has sent you two all the way from the USA to minister to us." They were in awe that we would travel thousands of miles to their little village in Uganda.

As we and all God's servants travel the globe in obedience to the Great Commission, we are never alone; we are accompanied by the One who gave the promise "I AM WITH YOU TO THE END OF THE AGE."

This is the Gospel we preach.

I trust and pray as you have read this book that it has been an encouragement to you.

God's richest blessing,

Keith Tipple

About the Author

Keith and his wife, Val, travel internationally, ministering in conferences, missions, and local churches.

Keith came to faith in Christ at the age of seventeen years. Initially called to the ministry as an evangelist, Keith traveled to many towns and cities around the UK, conducting evangelistic and church-planting missions. Keith and his wife, Val, have also planted and pastored several churches in the UK and are currently engaged in pastoral ministry in the USA.

They have a UK charitable trust called Ocean Wings, which helps to finance their trips to third-world countries. They minister regularly in Africa and have input into numbers of the village churches in Uganda.

Keith has also recorded two song albums one entitled *People Need the Lord* and the latest one, *My Dream Come True*.

Keith and Val have two sons Mark—who is married to Sian—and Paul—to Melissa—and they have nine grandchildren.

Keith Tipple can be contacted by 'Messenger' on Facebook and also by Ocean-Wings website,
www.ocean-wings.net